WORLD'S COMPACT
BIBLE DICTIONARY
AND
CONCORDANCE

edited by
Dan Penwell

WORLD
Bible Publishers, Inc.

A

AARON. Elder brother of Moses. He helped Moses in freeing the Israelites from bondage in Egypt. He became the first high priest and his descendants became the dominant priestly line. (Ex 4-7; 17.10-12; 24.9-14; 32.1-24; Lev 8.1-36; Num 12.1-16; 20.1-13; Heb 2.1-4; 9.4,7,25).

AARON'S ROD. A staff carried by Aaron. When thrown down before Pharaoh, it became a snake (Ex 7.9-15). It also budded as a sign of divine approval of Moses and Aaron (Num 17.1-10). It was preserved in the Ark of the Covenant (Heb 9.4).

ABBA. A term by which God is addressed—meaning Father. It was commonly used by children in addressing their father. (Mk 14.36; Rom 8.15; Gal 4.6).

ABEL. The second son of Adam. He was a keeper of sheep, but was later killed by his brother Cain. (Gen 4.2,8; Heb 11.4).

ABRAHAM. Known as the father of the Hebrew nation. His story begins at Gen 11.26. God made a covenant with Abraham which promised Abraham that his descendants would be greatly blessed (Gen 12.1-3). The family moved to Haran from which Abraham, at the age of 75, departed for Canaan. He is commended for having obeyed a divine command to undertake through faith this arduous journey (Heb 11:8). Because Sarah, his wife, was childless, Abraham had a son by her handmaid, Hagar, who bore Ishmael. Then to Sarah, when Abraham was one hundred years old and Sarah ninety, Isaac was born (Gen 21:1-4). The great test of Abraham's faith came when he was divinely commanded to sacrifice Isaac but he followed God's orders completely and was rewarded when the boy was saved (Gen 22:1-19; Rom 4; Gal 3.6-9; Heb 11.17-19).

ABSALOM. David's third son. He was physically attractive with beautiful long hair. He murdered his half-brother, Ammon, for disgracing his sister Tamor. He became more rebellious hoping to seize his father's throne, but was slain by Joab (2 Sam 13-18).

ADAM. The first man, made in God's own image (Gen 1.26,27), was created from dust and brought to life by God breathing into his nostrils the breath of life (Gen 2.7). He lived in the Garden of Eden and had dominion over all the animals. He tasted the forbidden fruit in disobedience which has had an eternal affect upon mankind (Rom 5.12-21).

ADULTERY. Unlawful sexual relations of a married person with one who is not a wife or husband. It is forbidden by the seventh commandment (Ex 20.14). Christ interpreted adultery to be not only the overt act, but also adulterous thoughts and emotions (Mt 5.27,28). Also used to signify disloyalty to the Lord through the worship of false gods (Hos 2.2-13).

ADVERSARY. In the OT means an accuser, one who takes a person into court with a charge. In the NT it refers to Satan or the Devil. (Josh 5.13; 1 Pet 5.8; 1 Tim 5.14).

ADVOCATE. One who acts in behalf of another. Jesus applied the word to the Holy Spirit, translated Comforter (Jn 14.26; 15.26; 16.7). Christ also is called the Advocate (1 Jn 2.1).

AHAB. A wicked king of Israel who ruled with his wicked wife, Jezebel (1 Kgs 16.28-22.4). Elijah condemned Ahab and Baal worship and at Mt. Carmel called on the Lord to bring down miraculous fire on his sacrifice (1 Kgs 18.36).

ALEXANDRIA. A famous city of Egypt founded by Alexander the Great in 332 B.C. The Jews from Alexandria helped in the stoning of Stephen (Acts 6.9). Apollos was an Alexandrian Jew (Acts 18.24, 25).

ALMS. The act of giving to the poor and needy (Acts 3.2,3,10; 10.2-4). Christ warns against almsgiving just for show and for compliments (Mt 6.2-4).

ALPHA and OMEGA. The first and last letters of the Greek alphabet. In reference to Christ, He is the beginning and end of all things (Rev 1.8, 11; 21.6; 22.13).

ALTAR. A structure of earth, stones, wood or bronze used for the offering of an animal sacrifice or upon which in-

4

cense was burned. Altars were often erected at spots where God had appeared or spoken. (Gen 8.20; Ex 20.24-25; 27.1-8, 30.1-10; Mt 5.23; Heb 13.10).

AMALEKITES. A nomadic desert tribe, descendants of Esaus' grandson, Amalek (Gen 36.12). They ranged the wastelands south and southeast of Canaan and were constant enemies of Israel from the time of their attack at Rephidim (Ex 17.8-16).

AMEN. Means "truly" or "surely". When people bound themselves with an oath they said, "Amen." It is spoken at the end of a prayer or pronouncement, by the speaker or listeners, to indicate readiness to commit oneself to what has been said. (1 Chr 16.36; Neh 5.13; Rom 9.5; 16.27; 1 Cor 14.16; 2 Cor 1.20).

AMOS. One of the twelve minor prophets and a herdsman who prophesied for the N. Kingdom of Israel. In his prophetic sermons he denounced the extravagant and unjust ways of God's people living in the N. Kingdom (Am 1-9; Lk 3.25).

ANANIAS. 1. An early Christian in Jerusalem. He and his wife, Sapphria, were dishonest in their dealings with the Christian community there (Acts 5.1-5). 2. A Christian in Damascus who baptized Paul (Acts 9.10-18). 3. A high priest in Jerusalem before whom Paul was tried (Acts 23.2).

ANDREW. One of the 12 apostles. He was a brother of Simon Peter and a fisherman with his brother. He brought Peter to Jesus (Jn. 1.35-42; Mt 4.18-19; 10.2).

ANGEL. An order of heavenly beings in the service of God (Ps 8.5; Heb 1.14; 2.7). They act as God's messenger (Gen 22.11; Ex 3.2) or intervene in moments of crisis (Gen 48.16; Mt 2.13; 28.2-3). There are also fallen angels (Mt 25.41; Rev 12.7-9).

ANOINT. To pour oil or ointment on the head or body of a person or object. Usually done to consecrate objects (Ex 29.36; 40.10) or persons (Ex 29.7; 1 Kgs 19.16) to the service of the Lord. Kings also were anointed (1 Sam 10.1;

16.1,12-13; 2 Sam 2.7; 2 Kgs 9.6). The words Messiah and Christ signify Anointed One. Christians are spiritually anointed (2 Cor 1.21).

ANTICHRIST. The word signifies against Christ or an enemy of Christ. Only John uses the term and he uses it to refer to a person, as well as an antagonistic attitude toward Christ (1 Jn 2.18,22; 4.3; 2 Jn 7). Jesus refers to "false Christs" (Mt 24.23-24) and Paul describes an "Antichrist" (2 Thess 2.3-12). The Antichrist will eventually be destroyed at Jesus' second coming.

ANTIOCH. 1. An important city of Syria on the river Orontes. When persecution of Christians at Jerusalem arose upon the martyrdom of Stephen, many fled to Antioch (Acts 11.19-26). It was here that the disciples were first called Christians. 2. A Greek city in Pisidia visited by Paul and Barnabas on their first missionary journey (Acts 13.14-52; 14.19-21).

APOLLOS. A eloquent Jew who was a disciple of John the Baptist and later a convert to Christianity. (Acts 18.24; 19.1; 1 Cor 1.12; 3.4-6,22; 16.12).

APOSTLE. One who is sent, a messenger. The name applied to the Twelve selected by Jesus to be with him, receive his training, be witnesses to the events of his life, and to preach the Gospel (Mt 4.18-22; 10.2-4; Lk 6.13-16). Paul claimed apostleship upon the basis of receiving his commission from the risen Lord (Rom 1.1; 1 Cor 9.1-2; 2 Cor 11.4-5).

AQUILA. A Christian Jew and tentmaker who, with his wife, Priscilla, worked with Paul and helped in the Christian training of Apollos (Acts 18.1-3, 18,26).

ARK. A large floating structure built by Noah out of gopher wood at the direction of the Lord. It is thought that the Ark was approximately 450 feet long, 75 feet wide and 45 feet high. Noah took at least two of each species of animal on board with him (Gen 6.14-8.19; Mt 24.38; Heb 11.7).

ARK OF THE COVENANT. An oblong chest that the Lord ordered Moses to make (Ex 25.10). It could be carried by two wooden poles inserted in four rings attached to the Ark's four corners. Within the Ark were the two tablets of stone on which were inscribed the law or covenant of God (Ex 25.21; Deut 10.3-5). Also inside was a pot of manna, Aaron's rod, and the book of the law (Ex 16.34; Deut 31.26; Heb 9.4). On the top were two cherubims of gold (Ex 25.10-22). The Ark was regarded as the seat or center of the presence of God (Ex 25.22; 1 Sam 4.4; Ps 99.5).

ASCENSION. Primary reference is to Christ's departure from earth into heaven (Lk 24.51; Acts 1.9-11; Eph 4.8-10). Elijah also ascended into heaven in a chariot of fire (2 Kgs 2.9-13). At the second coming of Christ, Christians will also ascend into heaven (1 Cor 15.51-52; 1 Thess 4.13-18).

ASHER. The eighth son of Jacob and second by Zilpah, the handmaid of Leah (Gen 30:13). The tribe of Asher was assigned the district that ran north from Carmel along the sea shore. To the east of it lay the tribes of Zebulun and Naphtali (Jos 19:24-31).

ASSYRIA. A land and people located about 500 miles NE of Jerusalem on the upper Tigris river. They are mentioned in the Bible chiefly for their warlike aggressions. They conquered Samaria and the N. Kingdom of Israel in 722 B.C. (Isa 7-8; 2 Kgs 17.3-5; 18.13-23).

ATHENS. The principal seat of Grecian civilization. Beautiful public buildings arrayed this city, such as the Parthenon. Philosophy, in a sense, began in Athens with such great thinkers as Socrates, Plato, and Aristotle. It was also the center of art, history, literature, and science. Paul preached a sermon in this city on Mars Hill (Acts 17.15-18.1).

ATONE, ATONEMENT. It is the means through the work of Christ bringing reconciliation between God and the sinner. The scriptural significance of atonement is expressed by the follwing: 1. Redemption, restored by ransom (Mt 20.28). 2. The purchase price (1 Cor 6.20) 3. A covering (Rom 4.7). 4. Bearing of penalty (Isa 53.4-6; Heb 9.28) 5. Securing the pardon of an offended God (Rom 5.10; 1 Jn 2.2-3) 6. Escaping the death sentence of the law through one upon whom the sentence fell (Gal 2.13).

ATONEMENT, DAY OF. Under the Jewish law, once a year on the tenth day of the seventh month, God required a day of fasting and repentance for individual sins and for the sins of the Hebrew nation. This was the only day that the High Priest entered into the Holy of Holies where he sprinkled blood from a slain goat as a sin offering for the people. On the head of the second goat he placed his hands and confessed the sins of the people and then sent it into the wilderness. The scape goat, symbolized the sin-bearer, Christ. (Lev 16; 23.26-32; Num 29.7-11; Heb 7.10; 9.7-28).

B

BAAL. The chief male deity of the Canaanites and Phoenicians. During the time of the judges, altars were built to him by the Israelites (Judg 2.13; 6.28-32). On Mt. Carmel, Elijah proposed a great test which completely discredited Baal and vindicated Jehovah (1 Kgs 16.31-32; 18.17-40) The worship of Baal was attended by immoral ceremonies and human sacrifice (Jer 19.5).

BABEL, TOWER OF. The huge brick tower erected in the plain of Shinar (Gen 11.1-9). The builders wanted to make a name for themselves. The Lord frustrated all their plans by confusing their speech.

BABYLON. The capital of Babylonia, built between the Tigris and Euphrates rivers. The tower of Babel was built in this area. Their greatest periods of history were during the reigns of Hammurabi (about 1800 B.C.) and Nebuchadnezzar (605-562 B.C.) who conquered Jerusalem and carried the Jews into captivity. Persia conquered Babylon in 538 B.C. The Babylon mentioned in (1 Pet 5.13) and in (Rev 14.8; 17.5; 18.2,10,21) many feel refer to Rome. The religion of Babylon involved many gods, but their gods had no moral qualities and did not demand any good ethical behavior by their followers.

BALAAM. A soothsayer who was summoned by King Balak of Moab to curse the Israelites who were invading the land. But when he received the word of God, he blessed, rather than cursed, the invaders (Num 24.1-14).

BAPTISM. A ceremonial act involving the use of water which symbolized washing and making pure in the sight of God. 1. Baptism of John (Mk 1.3-11; Jn 1.25-28; 3.23). 2. Baptism of Jesus (Mt 3.13-17; Mk 1.9-11). 3. Christian Baptism (Mt 28.18-20; Acts 2.37-41; 8.36-40; 10.47-48; 16.31-33; 22.16; Rom 6.3-5; Cor 2.12; 1 Pet 3.20-21). The importance of baptism is shown by the fact that the Lord Jesus himself submitted to it "to fulfill all righteousness" (Mt 3.15) and that he included it as a part of his great commission (Mt 28.18-20).

BARABBAS. A man held as a prisoner at the time of Jesus' trial who, rather than Jesus, was released at the wish of the Jews (Mt 27.16-26). He was called a bandit in one gospel (Jn 18.40), a murderer and leader of revolt in two others (Mk 15.7; Lk 23.19).

BARNABAS. He was one of the disciples who sold his holdings and brought the money to the apostles after the day of Pentecost (Acts 4.36,37). It was Barnabas who satisfied the doubting Jewish Christians of the genuineness of Paul's conversion and commended him to the brethren (Acts 9.27). The church at Antioch commissioned Paul and Barnabas to preach the Gospel to the Gentiles which resulted in the first missionary journey.

BARTHOLOMEW. One of the twelve apostles (Mt 10.3; Mk 3.18; Lk 6.14; Ac. 1.13). It is probably the surname of Nathanael (Jn 1.45,46).

BATHSHEBA. The wife of Uriah the Hittite. The black page of David's history was his adulterous relations with this woman. Uriah, who had been placed on the most dangerous position of the battlefront by the king's command, was slain, and David married Bathsheba. She became the mother of Solomon (2 Sam 11.3,4; 12.24; 1 Kgs 1.11).

BEAST. A large four-footed animal (Gen 1.30). In the Bible the word includes both wild and domesticated beasts (Lev 26.22; Jer 50.39; Mk 1.13). Daniel's prophecy of the four beasts are representative of the four great kingdoms (Dan 7.3,17,23). In Revelation antichrist and the false prophet are represented as beasts (Rev 13.1, 15.2, 17.8).

BEELZEBUL. The title of a heathen deity. To the Jews Beelzebul was the prince of evil spirits (Mt 10.25, 12.24; Mk 3.22; Lk 11.15-19). Jesus identifies him with Satan (Mt 12.26; Mk 3.23; Lk 11.18).

BENJAMIN. 1. The youngest son of Jacob. His mother was Rachel and Joseph was his full brother. His mother died at his birth (Gen 35.16-20). The strong paternal affection of Jacob for Benjamin is seen in his hesitancy in allowing him to go to Egypt with his other sons (Gen 43.1-17). Benjamin was also greatly loved by Joseph (Gen 43.29-34). 2. The tribe of Benjamin. When the land was divided, the section allotted to Benjamin was between Judah and Ephraim, the eastern limit of which was the Jordan (Josh 18.11-20).

BETHANY. A small town on the eastern slope of the Mount of Olives (Mk 11.1; 19.29) near the road from Jericho to Jerusalem. It was the town of Lazarus and his sisters, Mary and Martha (Jn 11.1, 12.1). It is the one place with which are associated more intimately than any other place the closing scenes of Jesus' life. In the house of Simon the leper Jesus was anointed (Mt 26.6-13; Mk 14.3). Here Jesus found retirement and rest and from near it he ascended to heaven.

BETHEL. An ancient town west of Ai and southwest of Shiloh (Gen 12.8; Ju 21.19). When he arrived in Palestine, Abraham pitched his tent here (Gen 13:3). The Canaanites called it Luz but Jacob named it Bethel because here he had his vision (Gen 28.19, 31.13) and it was the site of an altar he erected (Gen 35.1-15). It became a center of idolatry under Jeroboam (1 Kgs 12.29-33, 13:1.32). Because of this, it was denounced by the prophets (Jer 48.13; Hos 10.15; Am 3.14, 4.4).

BETHLEHEM. 1. A town of Judah, one of the oldest of Palestine, formerly called Ephrath and located five miles south of Jerusalem (Gen 35.16,19, 48.7; Mic 5.2). Rachel died and was buried near this town (Gen 35.16,19). It was the residence of Naomi, Boaz, Ruth, Obed, Jesse, and David (Ruth 1.19, 4.9-11,21,22; 1 Sam 16.1.4). It was the city of David (Lk 2.11) and the birthplace of Jesus (Mic 5.2; Mt 2.5).

BIRTHRIGHT. By this is meant the rights of the firstborn son. The father's rank and position as head of the family or tribe passed, at death, to the oldest son. By right he received a double portion of the father's property (Deut 21.15-17). The firstborn might sell his birthright (Gen 25.29,34; Heb 12.16).

BISHOP. The Greek word *episkopos*, an overseer, occurs first in Paul's injunction to the elders or presbyters of the church at Ephesus (Acts 20.17,28). In Paul's use of the word it is identical with elders and presbyters (Titus 1.5-7). Thus the words are used interchangeably. Paul specified his qualifications (1 Tim 3.1-7; Titus 1.7-9).

BLASPHEMY. Language by which God is defamed (Ps 74.18; Isa 52.5; Rom 2.24). The Mosaic law made this a capital offence punished by stoning (Lev 24.16). Jesus and Stephen, the first Christian martyr, were charged with blasphemy (Mt 9.3, 26.65,66; Jn 10:36; Acts 6.11).

BLESS, BLESSING. The bestowal of divine favor and benefits (Gen 1.22, 9.1-7, 39.5). It includes recognition of

11

God's goodness in a thankful and adoring manner (Ps 103.1; Mt 26.26; 1 Cor 11.24) and invoking God's favor upon another (Gen 27.4,12,27-29; Ps 129.8).

BLOOD. The blood represented life—the life is in the blood (Lev 17.11,14; Deut 12.23), and the life God regarded as sacred. The law announced that the shedding of man's blood would be punishable by death (Gen 9.6). The penalty of sin was the loss of life (Heb 9.22) as denoted by the death of animals used in the offerings for sin under the Mosaic law, and signified atonement (Lev 17.10-14; Deut 12.15,16), hence the expressions "the blood of Jesus Christ," or, "the blood of the Lamb" denote the atoning death of our Lord (1 Cor 10.16; Heb 9.14; 1 Pet 1.2,19; 1 Jn 1.7; Rev 12.11).

BRAZEN SERPENT. In the wilderness when the Israelites were bitten by fiery serpents, Moses was commanded to form a serpent of metal and place it upon a pole. Looking upon this with faith in the promise of God the Israelites were healed (Num 21.8,9). The lifting up of the brazen serpent on a pole in the wilderness was likened by Jesus to his death on the cross (Jn 3.14,15).

BREASTPLATE. 1. The breastplate of the Jewish high priest was a piece of embroidered cloth about ten inches square. Attached to it were twelve precious stones, each bearing the name of one of the twelve tribes (Ex 28.15-30). 2. A piece of armor to protect the breast of the warrior. It is used figuratively as the breastplate of righteousness (Isa 59.17; Eph 6.14; 1 Thess 5.8).

BRIDE, BRIDEGROOM. Words which, in addition to their usual meaning of persons newly married or about to be married, are, in the New Testament, used figuratively. Christ is represented as the Bridegroom and the church as his bride (Jn 3.29; Rev 21.9).

BURIAL. When a person died, friends came to the home and lamented the death of the deceased (Mk 5.38). This act was performed even by hired mourners (Jern 9.17). After the body was washed and bound with cloth (Mt

27.59; Jn 11.44), those who could afford it anointed the body with perfumes and spices (Jn 12.7, 19.39). The usual type of sepulchre was a cave (Gen 25.9,10; Mt 27.60).

C

CAESAR. After the death of the illustrious Gaius Julius Caesar, Augustus adopted the name as an official title as did practically every other Roman emperor thereafter for some two hundred years. While eleven Caesars (emperors) fall within the scope of New Testament times, only four are mentioned. Caesar Augustus (31 B.C.-A.D. 14) issued the decree that the world should be taxed (Lk 2.1). It was in the fifteenth year of Tiberius Caesar (A.D. 14-37) that John the Baptist began his ministry (Lk 3.1). In the days of Claudius Caesar (A.D. 41-54) the famine predicted by Agabus came to pass. Claudius also commanded all Jews, including Aquila and Priscilla, to leave Rome (Acts 11.28, 18.2). Nero Caesar (A.D. 54-68) is called merely Caesar in Phil 4.22. It was to Nero that Paul made his famous appeal (Acts 25.10-12).

CAESAREA. A seaport on the coast of Palestine on the road from Tyre to Egypt, about fifty miles from Jerusalem. It was built by Herod the Great and named in honor of Caesar Augustus. It was the Roman capital of Palestine. In this city Philip the Evangelist preached (Acts 8.40, 21.8) and it was here that the Roman centurion, Cornelius, lived, the first Gentile to come into the church (Acts 10.1,24, 11.11). In escaping from Jerusalem, Paul came to Caesarea (Acts 23.23,33) and remained a prisoner here for two years (Acts 25.1-13).

CAESAREA PHILIPPI. A city in the extreme northern part of Palestine at the foot of Mount Hermon, the scene of Christ's famous charge to Peter and the Transfiguration (Mt 16.13-20, 17.1-13).

CAIAPHAS. A Sadducee, the son-in-law of Annas (Jn 18.13) and high priest between A.D. 18 and 36. He demanded the death of Jesus (Mt 26.3-5; Jn 11.49-53, 18.14). Caiaphas participated in the trial of Peter and John (Acts 4.5-7).

CAIN. Eldest son of Adam and Eve, brother of Abel, whom he slew. An agriculturist, he made a thank offering while that of Abel was a blood offering. For this reason, his offering was rejected. Envious of his brother, he slew him, denied it and expressed no repentance. Exiled, he went to Nod where he married, his wife being one of the descendants of Adam. (Gen 4; Heb 11.4).

CALEB. He was one of the twelve spies sent from Kadesh to Canaan and strongly advised that the Israelites go forward and take the land. For this demonstration of faith in the Lord he and Joshua alone of all that company, who were over twenty years of age at the time, were permitted to enter the Promised Land (Num 13.2,6,30, 14.6,24,38; Josh 14.6,14).

CALF. A young cow or bullock, used for food (Gen 18.7) and for sacrificial purposes (Heb 9.12,19). It was one of the animals worshipped by the Egyptians which, no doubt, suggested to the Israelites at Sinai the making of a golden calf (Ex 32.4; Ps 106.19,20). When Jeroboam founded the northern kingdom he set up two golden calves, one at Bethel and one at Dan (1 Kgs 12.29).

CALVARY. The name is derived from the Latin *calvaria*, a skull (Lk 23.33). It corresponds to the Aramaic word *Golgotha* (Mt 27.33; Mk 15.22; Jn 19.17). Jerome offered as a possible explanaton of the name applied to the little hill the fact tht unburied skulls may have been there. Others suggest that it was so called because it was a place of execution. Still others suppose that the skull-shape of the hill gave rise to the name. It was outside the city wall and here the crucifixion of Christ occurred (Mt 27.33; Jn 19.17,20; Heb 13.11-13).

CAMEL. This animal was early known to the Egyptians (Gen 12.16). Called the ship of the desert, it has great powers of endurance, and while generally obedient, does not possess a sweet dispositon. The camel was used by Abraham and Jacob (Gen 12.16, 30.43) and a camel carried Joseph into Egypt (Gen 37.25). The camel was peculiarly adapted for desert travel (Ex 9.3; Judg 6.5; 1 Kgs 10.2).

CAMP. An encampment or stopping-place of a moving body of people or an army (Ex 14.19; 1 Sam 4.5; 2 Kgs 7.7). In their journeying through the wilderness the Hebrew camp was well-planned with the tabernacle in the center (Num 1.47-2.34, 3.14-39).

CANAAN 1. The son of Ham and grandson of Noah (Gen 10.6; 1 Chr 1.8). Canaan's sons were fathers of tribes in Syria and Palestine (Gen 10.15-19; 1 Chr 1:13-16). 2. By this name the country itself is sometimes understood. It was probably at first employed to denote the coast-line of Palestine (Num 13.29; Josh 11.3). It was then applied to the Jordan district and later to the whole country. It is called the Promised Land because it was promised to Abraham; the Holy Land because it was holy unto the Lord.

CAPERNAUM. A town on the northwestern coast of the Sea of Galilee (Mt 4.13-16; Lk 4.31; Jn 6.17-24). It was a city of importance, had its own synagogue, and was probably a military post (Mt 8.5-13; Lk 7.1-10). When Jesus was rejected at Nazareth, he made this his headquarters (Mt 9.1; Mt 2.1). It was the scene of many of his miracles and teachings. The centurion's servant, Peter's mother-in-law, a man sick of the palsy, a nobleman's son, and others were healed here (Mt 8.5-13; Mk 1.29-31, 2.1-13; Lk 7.1.10- Jn 4.46-54). In the synagogue and other places in the city Jesus taught (Mk 9.33-50; Jn 6.24-71). A custom station was located here and here Matthew, the taxgatherer, was called as one of the apostles (Mt 9.9-13; Mk 2.14-17). Jesus predicted the destruction of this unrepentant city (Mt 11.23, 24).

CAPTIVITY. Using the term in the sense of holding in bondage in a foreign land, the Egyptian bondage is the first of the captivities of the chosen people. But the two instances to which the word usually applies are the captivity of Israel and the captivity of Judah. In the case of the former, Assyria overthrew the kingdom in 722 B.C. After the besieging of Samaria by Shalmaneser, Sargon, in his first year, took it and carried away a great number of the people to Mesopotamia and Media (2 Kgs 17.5,6). The captivity of Judah was in three stages, the first in the reign of Jehoiakim in 606 B.C. (2 Chr 36.2-7; Dan 1.1-3) by Nebuchadnezzar who carried off Daniel and others. The second stage or deportation was eight years later (597 B.C.) in the reign of Jehoiachin when the king and about 11,000 of the people were taken to Babylon (2 Kgs 24.14-16). The third stage was the fall of Jerusalem in 586 B.C. when Nebuchadnezzar destroyed the city and carried away the people, leaving a remnant (2 Kgs 25.2-21). The captivity of Judah was predicted 150 years before it happened. It was declared that the captivity would last seventy years, and true to the promise of God, the Jews were released by Cyrus in 536 B.C.

CARPENTER. Carpentry as a distinct occupation is first mentioned in the Scriptures when carpenters of Tyre came to Jerusalem to build David's house (2 Sam 5.11). Various tools are mentioned, such as the hammer, nail, saw, and ax (Jer 10.4; Isa 10.15), and plane, compass, line (Is 44.13). Carpentry was Christ's occupation in Nazareth (Mk 6.3).

CAVE. The largest number of caves are to be found in limestone countries, such as Palestine, where the people often dwelt in them (Kgs 19.9). After the destruction of Sodom, Lot and his family found protection in a cave (Gen 19.30), the same was true of David and Elijah (1 Sam 22.1; 1 Kgs 19.9). They were used for burial purposes (Gen 23.1-20; Jn 11.38).

CENSUS. The Hebrews had a system of registering by tribe, family and house (Num 1.18). There were three specific numberings of Israel, the first at Sinai after leaving Egypt (Num 1). The second census was taken at the close of the wandering (Num 26.1-51). The third census was taken by David (2 Sam 24.1-9; 1 Chr 21.1-6). Shortly before the birth of Christ, Augustus ordered an enrollment of the people which brought Joseph and Mary to Bethlehem, the city of David (Lk 2.1).

CHARIOT. A two-wheeled vehicle used for both hostile and peaceful purposes. The body of the chariot rested on the axle and was open behind. The first mention of the chariot in the Bible is in connection with Joseph who was honored by being placed in the chariot of Pharaoh (Gen 41.43) and later rode in his own chariot (Gen 46.29). When used for military purposes, the strength of a nation was considered in terms of the number of its chariots. Pharaoh pursued the Israelites with 600, the Philistines had 30,000 (1 Sam 13.5). They were poorly adapted to the hills of Palestine, hence were not much used by Hebrews.

CHERUB, CHERUBIM. After the fall and expulsion from Eden, they guarded the tree of life (Gen 3.24). In the Holy of Holies, on the mercy seat of the ark, golden cherubim with overarching wings faced each other kneeling. They symbolized the presence of Jehovah in the midst of his people (Ex 25.18-20, 37.7-9; Num 7.89; Ps 80.1).

CHRIST. The title, The Anointed One, corresponds to the Messiah, the Hebrew name. It is the Greek translation of the Hebrew word. The Christ signifies the messiah of Old Testament prophecy (Mt 16.16,20; Mk 8.29; Jn 1.41). Jesus, the personal name of Christ, given at his birth, is often used with Christ—Jesus Christ—so that the word Christ becomes practically a part of the proper name (Jn 1.17; Acts 11.17; Rom 5.1).

CHRISTIAN. The word signifies a follower of Christ. The name was first applied to the disciples at Antioch in Syria about 43 A.D. (Acts 11.26). The disciples were called *disciples* (Acts 9.26; 11.29), *believers* (Acts 5.14). We are simply told that the disciples were called Christians first in Antioch. Some authorities are of the opinion that it was applied by foes rather than friends. The name came into use very slowly, and was not given until about thirteen years after the founding of Christianity. The word is used three times in the New Testament (Acts 11.26, 26.38; 1 Pet 4.16).

CHURCH. It is the rendering in the New Testament of the Greek word *Ekklesia*, the original meaning of which was that of an assembly of citizens convened by a civil authority. The Greek word is employed by the New Testament to denote the body of Christian people, a Christian community, the followers of Christ. In different cities believers formed themselves into a church, and thus churches signified the various communities of this nature (Acts 9.31, 15.41; Rom 16.4; 1 Cor 7.17). Those truly invited to Christ by saving faith in him are of the invisible Church and may come into fellowship with an external body (1 Cor 1.2, 12.12; Col 1.24; 1 Pet 2.9,10).

CIRCUMCISION. This was not an exclusively Jewish rite, but for the Hebrews it had special significance in that it was divinely instituted—being the seal of God's covenant with Abraham and his descendants (Gen 17.1-14,21). It was performed on the male child when he was eight days old (Lev 12.3). In being admitted to the Jewish commonwealth all male foreigners were required to receive this rite (Gen 34.14-17,22; Ex 12.48). The term "uncircumcised," as applied to other nations, was a term of reproach (Judg 14.3; 1 Sam 17.26,36; 2 Sam 1.20).

CLOUD, PILLAR OF. A miraculous cloud in the form of a pillar, the symbol of the Lord's presence. It preceded the Israelites in the wilderness to guide them by day. At night it assumed the form of, or yielded its place to, a pillar of fire (Ex 13.21,22; Neh 9.19). It was the means by which God revealed his presence to Israel during the marching of the Exodus (Num 12.5; Deut 31.15).

CORNERSTONE. The stone that binds together the sides of a building (Ps 118.22; Isa 28.16; Zech 4.7). It was a term often applied to Christ (Rom 9.33; Eph 2.20; 1 Pet 2.6) who was also called the head of the corner (Mt 21.42; 1 Pet 2.7).

COUNCIL. This word usually denotes the Sanhedrin, the highest legislative body of the Jews. It was composed of 71 members including the high priest who was its president. It had the power of life and death (Mt 26.3,57; Acts 4.5, 6,15, 6.12,15) but could not execute the sentence of death, which was the prerogative of Rome. Jesus was tried before this body (Mt 26.59; Mk 14.55; Jn 11.47), as were the apostles (Acts 4.5,6,15, 5.21,27), Stephen (Acts 6.12), and Paul (Acts 22.30, 23.15, 24.20).

COVENANT. An agreement or compact (Gen 21.27.32; 1 Sam 18.3, 23.18; 1 Kgs 20.34). God made a covenant with Adam and Eve, promising divine favor in return for obedience (Gen 2.16,17). God covenanted with Noah that he would survive the deluge (Gen 6.18) and that there would never again be such a flood (Gen 9.12-16). Other divine covenants were with Abraham (Gen 13.17; 17.2,4,7,11,13, 14; 2 Kgs 13.23; Acts 7.8; Rom 4.13,17); with the Israelites (Ex 31.16). There was also given a new covenant of a more spiritual nature (Jer 31.31-34; Heb 8.8-11), designed for all peoples (Mt 28.19,20; Acts 10.44-47) with Christ as the Mediator (Heb 8.6-13; 9.1, 10.15-17, 12.24), to be administered by the Holy Spirit (Jn 7.39; Acts 2.32,33; 2 Cor 3.6-9).

CREATION. The Bible opens with the doctrine that God is the author of creation, that he caused to be that which did not previously exist. The things created: the heavens and the earth, all forms of life, the heavenly bodies, the elements (Gen 1; Ps 51.10, 148.5; Isa 40.26; Am 4.13). The general account is given in Gen 1.1-2.3. The second chapter of Genesis gives a more detailed account of the creation of Adam and Eve. The doctrine that all things were created by the mighty power of God is clearly taught in the Old Testament (Ps 33.6-9, 90.2, 104.1-14, 30; Isa 40.26-28, 42.5, 44.24, 45.7-13.18; Jer 51.15; Am 4.13). The

New Testament further unfolds this teaching by revealing the creative work of Christ, the Word (Jn 1.1-3; Col 1.15-18; Heb 1.1-3,10).

CROSS. Crucifixion was common among some nations of antiquity. The cross consisted of two pieces of wood, fastened together at right angles, upon which the victim was placed. To the upper part of the cross, above the head of the victim, a sign bearing his name or crime was placed (Mt 27.37; Mk 15.26; 19.19). Crucifixion was regarded with the same feeling of horror that is associated with *gallows* today (Jn 19.31; 1 Cor 1.23; Gal 3.13; Heb 12.2). Paul gloried in the cross of Christ because it signified the atoning work of the Saviour (Gal 6.14; Eph 2.16; Col 1.20).

CROWN. A headdress for ornamentation or denoting high position worn by high priests (Ex 29.6; 39.30; Ezek 21.26). On it was inscribed, "Holiness to the Lord." It was a gold plate attached with blue lace. The royal crown was of gold (Ps 21.3) and was often studded with gems (2 Sam 12.30; Zech 9.16). At his crucifixion a crown of thorns was placed on Jesus' head in derision of his alleged claims (Mt 27.29). Paul wrote to Timothy of the crown of righteousness (2 Tim 4.8) and Christ is described as being crowned with glory and honor (Heb 2.9).

CRUCIFIXION. A method of capital punishment in which the victim was affixed alive to a cross. It was a common practice of ancient nations. Alexander the Great crucified one thousand Tyrians and Antiochus Epiphanes used crucifixion as punishment for Jews who refused to renounce their religion. The Jews used stoning as their mode of capital punishment but insisted that the Romans crucify Jesus. The Saviour was first scourged (Mt 27.26; Mk 15.15) and then was compelled to carry the cross to the place of execution (Jn 19.17). Death to the victims was hastened by breaking their legs (Jn 19.31-33). Often a potion was given the victims to deaden pain but this was refused by Jesus (Mt 27.34).

CYPRUS. An island of the Mediterranean about forty miles from the coast of Cilicia, having about 3,584 square miles. It is first mentioned in the New Testament as the native place of Barnabas (Acts 4.36). During the persecution, following the martyrdom of Stephen, Christians went to Cyprus. Paul and Barnabas, on the first missionary journey, visited it (Acts 13.4) and afterwards it was visited by Barnabas and Mark (Acts 15.39).

CYRUS. The founder of the Persian empire. Isaiah names him as the divine instrument for the release of the Jews from the Babylonian Exile (Isa 44.28, 45.1-14). In 536 B.C., a few years after the fall of Babylon, Cyrus issued a proclamation which permitted the Jews to return to their own land. He restored the sacred vessels of the Temple which had been carried to Babylon by Nebuchadnezzar (Ezra 1.1-11, 5.13,14, 6.3).

D

DAMASCUS. This ancient city was the most important of Syria. It lay in a fertile plain, about thirty miles in diameter, which was watered by the Pharpar and Abana Rivers (2 Kgs 5.12). In 63 B.C. the city became a Roman province. There were Jewish synagogues in Damascus and near this city Paul was converted (Acts 9.2,3,10, 22.6, 10,11).

DAN. 1. Fifth son of Jacob by Bilhah, Rachel's maid (Gen 30.5,6). Jacob foretold the future of the tribe which would descend from him (Gen 49.16,17). 2. The tribe which descended from the above.

DANIEL. A heroic Jewish youth taken as a captive to Babylon, where he was educated and prepared for royal service. With God's help, he interpreted the king's dreams. Eventually he was made a ruler and chief of the governors of Babylon. Later he refused to pray to the king and was thrown in a lion's den. The dreams and visions of Daniel have great historical and prophetic significance. The story, prophecies and dreams are related throughout the 12 chapters of the book of Daniel.

DAVID. The son of Jesse and one of the greatest men of the Bible. 1. *His youth in Bethlehem.* He was the youngest of eight brothers (1 Sam 16.10,11, 17.12-14). and is described as ruddy and beautiful in appearance (1 Sam 16.12). He was a shepherd over his father's sheep (1 Sam 16.11, 17.34-36) and was a talented harpist. 2. *His relations with Saul.* David became armourbearer and musician to Saul and a valiant warrior, as was shown by his single-handed defeat of the giant, Goliath (1 Sam 16:14-18,21, 17.32-58). 3. *His life as fugitive and outlaw.* Fleeing from Saul, David took refuge in the cave of Adullam (1 Sam 22.1) and, gathering a band of six hundred men, he defeated the Philistines at Keilah (1 Sam 23.1-5). Twice he refused opportunities to take Saul's life (1 Sam 24,26). 4. *King of all Israel.* Israel proposed that both kingdoms be reunited under David (2 Sam 5.1-5). The ark was brought to Jerusalem (2 Sam 6.1-23). Worship of the Lord was organized (1 Chr 15,16). David sinned greatly in making Bath-sheba his wife but repented deeply (2 Sam 11.1-12,24; Ps 51). David died after having reigned forty years, turning over the kingdom to his son, Solomon (1 Kgs 2.10,11).

DEACON. A member of the early church and later a church official who was charged with a special kind of ministry. The Twelve Apostles appointed seven deacons to administer the charitable funds of the church (Acts 6.1-6). Eventually the deacon came to be regarded as a church official alongside the bishop (Phil 1.1). His qualifications are explicitly stated (1 Tim 3.8-13).

DEAD SEA. It is nearly fifty miles long and nine to ten miles wide and has a level of about 1,300 feet below the Mediterranean. Since it has no outlet, its saltiness is about four times that of the ocean.

DELILAH. The Philistine woman who lived in the valley of Sorek (Judg 16.4-18). She was paid a large sum of money by Philistine chiefs to induce Samson to disclose to her the secret of his strength.

DEMAS. A fellow-laborer of Paul (Col 4.14; Phil 24). Unwilling to endure privation, he deserted Paul and went to Thessalonica (2 Tim 4.10).

DEMETRIUS. A silversmith at Ephesus whose business of making silver shrines of the goddess, Diana, was threatened by Paul's teachings. Demetrius stirred up a riot, whereupon Paul left Ephesus (Acts 19.24-41).

DEMON. One of the lower order of spiritual beings who left their "first estate." Satan is the prince of demons (Mt 9.34; Lk 11.15). There were many demons but one devil. Persons possessed by demons suffered from diseases and were tortured (Lk 4.33, 8.30; Jn 7.20). They are represented as speaking (Mk 1.23,24, 5.7), and as being distinct from those whom they possessed (Mt 8.31). They exhibited unusual knowledge (Mk 1.24).

DEVIL. The word is used frequently in the sense of Satan, the chief of the fallen spirits (Lk 10.18; 2 Pet 2.4, Rev 12.7-9). It is generally believed that the sin by which he fell from his former state was pride (1 Tim 3.6). He is the enemy of God and of the divine order (Mt 13.38,39; Rev 12.17). He was the tempter of Adam and Eve (Gen 3.1-15; 2 Cor 11.3), Jesus (Mt 4.1-11), and man (Jn 13.2; Acts 13.9,10). He is a murderer and liar (Jn 8.44; Rev 20.10). Peter represents him as a devouring lion (1 Pet 5.8). He is subtle but can be resisted and put to flight (Eph 4.27, 6.11-16; Jas 4.7). Jesus came to destroy his works (Gen 3.15; 1 Jn 3.8).

DISCIPLE. Meaning followers of a teacher, such as the disciples of Paul or of Christ. (Mt 10.24; Lk 14.26,27; Jn 4.1, 6.66), the term is used of the apostles (Mt 5.1, 10.1, 12.1).

DIVINATION. The art that claims that things of the future may be ascertained by certain signs or be communicated by a form of inspiration. Diviners were found in great numbers among heathen nations (Deut 18.9-12; 1 Sam

6.2; Ezek 21.21; Dan 2.2; Acts 16.16). The Israelites were forbidden to consult such soothsayers (Lev 20.6,27; Deut 18.10; Isa 2.6; 10.2).

DREAM. A series of images, thoughts, or emotions occurring during sleep. Throughout the Bible significance is attached to dreams (Gen 37.6,9; Judg 7.13; Dan 2.28, 7.1; Mt 1.20, 2.12,13,19). They were not infrequently regarded as genuine communications from God (Job 33.14-17; Jer 23.28).

DRUNKENNESS. The state characterized by being drunken or intoxicated. Its earliest Biblical mention is in connection with Noah (Gen 9.21). Warnings against strong drink are frequent in the Bible (Lev 10.9; 23.29-32). Drunkenness is a reproach (Rom 13.13; Gal 5.21; Eph 5.18; 1 Thess 5.7).

E

EDEN. The name applied to the Garden of Eden. There has been considerable controversy over its location but it is generally conceded that the Euphrates and Tigris are branches of the river that flowed through it (Gen 2.8,10). It is here that Adam and Eve were tempted, ate of the tree of knowledge, and were expelled from the garden (Gen 3.4-6).

ELDER. An officer who was head of a family or tribe (Judg 8.14,16; 1 Kgs 8.1-3). The name signified that he was a man of mature age. The elder exercised authority over the people (Deut 27.1; Ezra 10.8) and in matters of state, elders represented the people (Ex 3.18; Judg 11.5-11; 1 Sa 8.4). In the early Christian church such designations as elder, presbyter and bishop, if not strictly synonymous, were interchangeable (Acts 20.17; Titus 1.5,7). Elders were in the church at Jerusalem in A.D. 44 (Acts 11.30). On his first journey Paul appointed elders in every church (Acts 14.23). They cooperated with the apostles in the government of the church (Acts 15.2,4,6,22, 16.4).

They had spiritual care of the congregation (1 Tim 3.5, 5.17; Titus 1.9; 1 Pet 5.1-4).

ELI. High priest at the temple of Shiloh during the eleventh century B.C. He helped to train Samuel (1 Sam 1.9, 24-28). Although a man of great piety, he was unable to control his sons, Hophni and Phinehas, whose conduct was disgraceful (1 Sam 2.23-25, 3.13). God's denunciation of Eli and his house was spoken through the boy Samuel and through an unnamed prophet (1 Sam 2.27-36, 3.11-18).

ELIJAH. One of the greatest of the prophets, a Tishbite who lived in Gilead (1 Kgs 17.1). Little else is known of his origin. He appeared suddenly during the reign of Ahab (about 876-854 B.C.) to denounce the king and his wife Jezebel, for their idolatry and crimes. His purpose was to save Israel from the worship of Baal. On Mount Carmel he succeeded in discrediting the 400 prophets of Baal by causing a fire to burn on a water-soaked altar (1 Kgs 18.19-46). Following the scene on Mount Carmel, Elijah fled from the furious Jezebel to Mount Horeb, where, like Moses, he was divinely sustained for forty days (Ex 24.18, 34.28; Deut 9.9, 18; 1 Kgs 19.8). When Naboth was murdered at the instigation of Jezebel, Elijah met Ahab and declared the judgments of God upon him (1 Kgs 21.1-29). Like Enoch, Elijah was translated to heaven without dying. Elijah appeared with our Lord in the transfiguration (Mt 17.4; Lk 9.30). The last two verses of the Old Testament predict that Elijah will appear on earth before the dreadful day of the Lord (Mal 4.5,6), while the New Testament explains this in terms of John the Baptist, who, in some respects, was like Elijah (Mt. 3.4; Mk 1.6; Lk 1.17).

ELIZABETH. A descendant of Aaron, wife of Zachariah and mother of John the Baptist. An angel revealed to her the fact that she was to be the mother of the forerunner of Christ. She was a kinswoman of Mary, mother of Jesus (Lk 1.5-45).

ELISHA. He was plowing his father's field when Elijah found him and appointed him his successor (1 Kgs

19.16,19). Leaving his home, Elisha joined Elijah and was with him when Elijah was transported to Heaven (2 Kgs 2.1-18). Included among his miracles: causing water to spring from barren land (2 Kgs 2.19-22); the death of the children who mocked his bald head (2 Kgs 2.23-25); the increase in the oil to pay the widow's debts (2 Kgs 4.1,7); the son restored to life (2 Kgs 4.8-37); the feeding of the hundred men (2 Kgs 4.42-44); the healing of Naaman (2 Kgs 5.1-19); and blinding the Syrian soldiers who pursued him (2 Kgs 6.17-23).

EPAPHRAS. A member of the Colossian church and possibly the founder of it. He came to Paul at Rome during his first imprisonment. In Paul's epistle to that church he joined the apostle in sending salutations (Col 1.7,8, 4.12). Paul speaks of him as "my fellow prisoner" (Phil 23).

EPAPHRODITUS. A Christian sent with gifts from the church at Philippi to Paul, then a prisoner at Rome. Epaphroditus became ill while there but, upon recovery, he returned to Philippi taking with him Paul's epistle to that church (Phil 2.25-30, 4.18).

EPHRAIM. 1. Joseph's younger son. He was born after Joseph became prime minister of Egypt (Gen 41.45-52). When Jacob placed his right hand on the head of Ephraim, the younger son, he explained to Joseph that Ephraim would be the greater and would be the ancestor of a multitude of peoples. The descendants of the two sons were to be regarded as two tribes (Gen 48.8-20). 2. The tribe of Ephraim. In the division of the land, on the south of Ephraim was Benjamin, on the north Manasseh, and on the west Dan.

EPISTLE. A letter, particularly one with a formal style and containing a specific teaching or doctrine. Twenty-one of the 27 books of the New Testament are in the form of formal letters, or epistles. Usually they were addressed to individuals, groups, or churches. With two exceptions they open with a statement as to authorship or destination. About a dozen such letters are attributed to Paul.

Four others claim as their authors James, Peter, and Jude. Three are ascribed to John. The author of the epistle to the Hebrews is not named. These letters were written to meet definite needs, such as correcting the conditions of the churches, teaching Christian doctrine, or refuting heretical ideas.

ESAU. The oldest son of Isaac and Rebekah; a hunter. He sold his birthright to his brother, Jacob, for a mess of red pottage. For this he was given the name Edom which means red (Gen 25.27-34; Heb 12.16, 17). Esau was cheated from receiving the blessing of his father by the deception of Jacob and Rebekah. Esau's fury at this caused Jacob to flee to Mesopotamia (Gen 27.1-31.55). However, he treated Jacob kindly when he returned from Mesopotamia (32.3-33.15). His descendants were called Edomites (Deut 2.4,12,22).

ESTHER. The beautiful daughter of Abihail, a Benjamite (Esth 2.15). After being brought up by her uncle, Mordecai, she became the favorite wife of King Ahasuerus.

EUNUCH. A chamberlain, one who had charge of beds and bedchambers. Those chosen for the office were rendered impotent (Isa 56.3; Mt 19.12). This class frequently rose to high position and considerable authority. The treasurer of Candace, queen of Ethiopia, was a eunuch and was converted to Christianity (Acts 8.27-38).

EUPHRATES. One of the great rivers of Asia, the Euphrates rises in northeast Turkey, flows through Syria and Iraq, and empties into the Persian Gulf. It is 1,780 miles long. About 90 miles above its mouth it is joined by the Tigris. In ancient times the greatest city along its banks was Babylon. It was the eastern boundary of the land of Israel (Gen 15.18; 1 Kgs 4.21,24).

EVANGELIST. In the early church a class of men who went from place to place preaching the gospel. They were distinct from apostles, pastors, and teachers (Eph 4.11). Philip, who was instrumental in the conversion of the eunuch, was an evangelist (Acts 6.5, 8.5,26, 21.8). Paul enjoined Timothy to do the work of an evangelist (2 Tim 4.5).

EVE. The mother of all living (Gen 3.20); fashioned from a rib taken from the side of Adam (Gen 2.18-22). She and Adam were forbidden to eat the fruit of a particular tree, as a test of their obedience. Under the influence of Satan, the serpent induced Eve to violate the command and she induced Adam to do likewise (Gen 3.1-24; 2 Cor 11.3; 1 Tim 2.13).

EXODUS. The departure of the Israelites from their life of bondage in Egypt. They were led by Moses. This marks the beginning of the history of the Israelites as a nation. They left Rameses in Goshen and traveled to Succoth (Ex 12.37). The shortest route to Canaan would have been through the land of the Philistines. But, because they might encounter war by this route, they were led instead through the wilderness by the Red Sea (Ex 13.17,18). At Pi-hahiroth they passed through the Red Sea, which had been made dry for them (Ex 14.1-31). They then entered the wilderness of Shur (Ex 15.22; Num 33.8). and traveled along the coast of the Red Sea toward Mount Sinai. They reached the land of Canaan 40 years after they left Egypt.

EZEKIEL. One of the major prophets, a Zadokite priest and the son of Buzi (Ezek 1.3). He was among the captives taken by Nebuchadnezzar to Babylonia in about 597 B.C. (2 Kgs 24.10-16).

EZRA. A famous priest, reformer, scribe, and student of law, who lived during the time of the Babylonian captivity. Artaxerxes, the Persian king, permitted Ezra and a group of his followers to return to Jerusalem. When he arrived there, he found religious affairs at a low ebb. He thereupon initiated reforms, among them the decree that foreign wives be divorced (Ezra 10.9-17). Ezra disappears from the Biblical narrative here although as Ezra, the scribe, he reappears later to read the law of Moses (Neh 8.1-13).

F

FAITH. Faith is the belief or trust in things unseen (2 Cor 4.18, 5.17; Heb 11.1). In a religious sense faith is applied particularly to God or to Christ, the author and finisher of our faith (Mk 11.22-24; Jn 3.16,33-36, 20.31; Heb 12.2; 1 Jn 5.9-14). Belief generally indicates intellectual assent to the evidence establishing the claims of the Scriptures (1 Cor 15.12-17; 1 Tim 6.20,21; 2 Tim 2.18). Faith implies a confidence or trust which comes after the belief has been established (Mt 13.3-17; Lk 8.10; Jn 8.30-32; 1 Cor 2.9-16).

FAMINE. Crop failure was the chief cause of famines in Biblical times, although they also occurred in cities under seige. Notable famines in the Scriptures took place in the time of Abraham (Gen 12.10), Isaac (Gen 26.1), Joseph in Egypt (Gen 41.27-57), Jacob (Gen 42.1-3, 47,1-13), judges (Ruth 1.1), David (2 Sam 21.1), Elijah (1 Kgs 17.1-18.46), Elisha (2 Kgs 4.38, 8.1), in the reign of Claudius, A.D. 41-54 (Acts 11.28), at the siege of Samaria (2 Kgs 6.24-7.20), and at the siege of Jerusalem (2 Kgs 25.1-3).

FAST. The first instance of voluntary fasting is that of David when he refused to eat during the sickness of his child (2 Sam 12.22). In the later books are recorded many instances of fasting (Ezra 8.21; Neh 9.1; Esth 4.3; Ps 69.10; Dan 6.18, 9.3). It signified a state of humility before God because of sin (1 Sam 7.6; 1 Kgs 21.9,12). The Pharisees fasted twice a week (Lk 18.12), a formalism criticized by Jesus (Mt 6.16,17).

FEAST. Feasts are often mentioned in the Bible. They celebrated important or joyful events. Three annual feasts were required by Mosaic law. The first was the *Passover*, on the fourteenth day of the first month, which was followed the next day by the feast of unleavened bread (Lev 23.5,6). The second annual festival was the *Feast of Weeks*, later called *Pentecost*, occurring fifty days after

Passover (Lev 23.15,16; Acts 2.1). The third festival was the *Feast of Tabernacles*, on the fifteenth day of the seventh month. Lasting for seven days, it commemorated the period in the wilderness (Lev 23.34-44). All adult males were required to appear on these three occasions (Ex 23.17; Deut 16.16). Another important religious feast is the Feast of Purim celebrating the deliverance of the Jews at the time of Esther (Esth 9.21-28).

FESTUS. The successor of Felix as procurator of Judea (Acts 24.10,27) about A.D. 60. He listened to Paul's defence in the presence of Agrippa II. Festus was satisfied as to Paul's innocence but proposed that he be tried in Jerusalem. This was unwise and Paul asserted his right to appeal to Caesar (Acts 25.1-26.32).

FIG. A tree of Palestine and its edible fruit. Some of these trees grow to a height of fifteen feet. Looking like a small green knob, the young fruit appears in the early spring before the leaf buds. This fact is alluded to by Jesus in the parable about the barren fig tree (Mk 11.13,14).

FIRSTBORN. God claimed the firstborn, both of men and animals. In the tenth plague of Egypt the firstborn of the Egyptians were slain and by the sprinkling of blood the firstborn of the Hebrews were preserved, hence they were dedicated to Jehovah (Ex 12.12,13,23,29). Every firstborn male was presented to the Lord at the sanctuary (Num 18.15; Lk 2.22).

FLOOD. The deluge at the time of Noah which, according to the Scriptures, was divine judgment for the wickedness of man (Gen 6.5-7.24). Only the righteous Noah, his family, and a large number of animals were permitted to escape by riding out the flood in an ark. The rain began on the seventeenth day of the second month and on the seventeenth day of the seventh month the ark rested on the mountains of Ararat (Gen 8.1-4). Three months later the tops of the mountains appeared. Noah left the ark on the twenty-seventh day of the second month of the new year. The flood had lasted about a year (Gen 8.14-19).

FOOD. The diet of the Hebrews in Palestine was almost entirely vegetarian. Meat was eaten occasionally by the rich. Mosaic law stated that only animals which chewed the cud and had cloven hoofs were edible. Serpents, creeping things, and fish without scales were forbidden (Lev 7.26, 11.10, 17.10-14; Deut 12.16). Bread was the staple of the table. Lentils were also important. Onions, leeks, cucumbers, and garlic were used as relishes. Edible fruits were figs, olives, grapes, pomegranates, almonds, and melons. Foods derived from the animal kingdom were honey, locusts, milk, curds, meat, and fish.

FOOL. The word is used for two purposes—to indicate one who is stupid and unwise (1 Sam 26.21) and to indicate one who disregards God or does not believe in him (Ps 14.1, 92.6; Prov 14.9; Jer 17.11).

G

GABRIEL. A heavenly messenger high in rank among the angels. He was sent to Daniel to interpret a vision received by the prophet (Dan 8.16-27). Centuries afterwards he appeared to Zacharias to announce the birth of John the Baptist (Lk 1.11-22) and at Nazareth he declared to Mary her great distinction and honor (Lk 1.26-31).

GAD. 1. The son of Jacob and Zilpah, Leah's handmaid (Gen 30.10,11). The tribe was commended by Moses (Deut 33.20,21). 2. The tribe of Gad (Num 1.14; Deut 27.13). The tribe was assigned territory east of the Jordan.

GAIUS. A Roman name sometimes written, Caius. 1. Gaius of Macedonia was a traveling companion of Paul. In the riot in Ephesus he was seized by the Ephesians (Acts 19.29). 2. Gaius of Derbe accompanied Paul on his last journey to Asia (Acts 20.4). 3. Gaius of Corinth, Paul's host, was baptized by Paul (Rom 16.23; 1 Cor 1.14). He was probably the same as Gaius of Derbe. 4. The Gaius to whom John addressed his third epistle (3 Jn 1).

GALILEE. In New Testament times Galilee was one of the three provinces of Palestine. It was located in the northern part. Many Gentiles lived here as was indicated by the expression "Galilee of the nations" (Isa 9.1; Mt 4.15). Jesus was raised in Galilee, and performed several miracles there.

GALILEE, SEA OF. It is fed by the river Jordan. Its greatest length is about twelve miles and its greatest breadth about seven and a half miles. Its surface is about 680 feet below the Mediterranean. It was the center of a busy, industrious life. A chief industry was fishing.

GAMALIEL. A doctor of the law, a Pharisee, and a member of the Sanhedrin. He was held in high regard by the Jews. Paul received his training in the law under this man (Acts 22.3). Gamaliel opposed the persecution of the apostles (Acts 5.34-39).

GAZA. One of the five main cities of the Philistines, the scene of many struggles between the Israelites and the Philistines (Josh 13.3; Judg 1.18; 1 Sam 6.17). It is located on the Mediterranean Sea not far from the desert. It was the scene of many exploits in Samson's career, including the destruction of the temple of Dagon (Judg 16:23.31). Dire predictions were made about the city by the prophets (Jer 47.1,5; Am 1.6,7; Zeph 2.4; Zech 9.5).

GENEALOGY. It was very essential that ancestral records be kept by the Jews to safeguard succession to the throne, the high priesthood, tribal headship, and head of the father's house. From the earlier days of their nation such records were kept (Num 1.2,18; 1 Chr 5.7,17; Mt 1.1-17; Lk 3.23-38).

GENERATION. Biblical usage of this term varies according to different periods through which the Hebrews lived. In the patriarchal age, a generation was reckoned at a century—the 400 years of the sojourn in Egypt were referred to as four generations (Gen 15.13-16). In other passages the word refers to a period of about thirty-five to forty years (Job 42.16).

GENTILES. The Hebrew word meaning nations, i.e., political and religious groups other than Israel (Judg 4.2, 13,16). Sometimes the word is translated nations (Gen 10.5,20; Neh 5.8; Ps 2.1). The word usually had an unfavorable meaning.

GERIZIM. It was on Mount Gerizim that Abraham was directed to sacrifice Isaac, according to the Samaritans. At the base of the mountain is the well of Jacob (Jn 4.6) and a little to the north is the tomb of Joseph (Josh 24.32). After entering the valley, Moses directed that the law be read from Mount Gerizim and Mount Ebal (Deut 11.29; Josh 8.33).

GETHSEMANE. A garden traditionally located near the foot of Mount Olivet (Lk 22.39). At the time of Christ it contained many olive trees but these were probably cut down in the first Christian century by Titus. This garden was often visited by Jesus and his disciples (Jn 18.2). It was here that, betrayed by Judas, Jesus was taken prisoner by soldiers and priests.

GIDEON. He lived in Ophrah (Judg 6.11-15). By clever strategy he managed to defeat the Midianites with only a very small army (Judg 7.19-24). He was probably the greatest of the judges.

GILGAL. The first camp of the Israelites after they crossed the Jordan., It was in the plain of Jericho. Here twelve stones were set up as a memorial (Josh 4.19,20) and here the first Passover was celebrated in Canaan (Josh 5.9,10).

GIRDLE. An important article of dress in the East. It was used by both sexes. Made of leather (Kgs 1.8; Mt 3.4), this belt was sometimes embroidered with silver and gold thread (Dan 10.5; Rev 1.13, 15.6). It was adorned at times with precious stones. The military girdle worn about the waist was used to carry the sword (Judg 3.16; 2 Sam 20.8).

GLEANING. The *poor law* of the Hebrews required that the gleaning of the fields, fruit trees, and vineyards be left to the poor. What produce was not removed by the reapers was taken by the gleaners (Judg 8.2; Ruth 2.7,9,16; Isa

17.6). The law required that no field or vineyard be gleaned by its owner (Lev 19.9,10, 23.22; Deut 24.19).

GOAT. In Palestine and Syria there are two or three varieties of the ordinary goat. Goats and sheep were under the care of the same shepherd (Gen 27.9, 30.32), but were kept apart (Mt 25.32). Cloth was made from the hair (Ex 25.4, 35.26). It provided milk and its flesh was eaten (Lev 7.23; Deut 14.4). It was used as a burnt and sin offering (Ex 12.5; Lev 1.10; Pa 66.15; Heb 9.12).

GOD. The Bible opens with the fact of God. The Bible is the record of the revelation of God. By no philosophical process does the Bible reach the conception of God. The Greek philosopher worked from the world and its phenomena up to God. The Grecian philosophical procedure was not that of the Hebrew thinker. The Hebrew did not think from the world to God; he began with God as the source, and the world and all things followed.

Unity of God. There is but one self-existing being. The Bible reveals God to us as one, and the only God. There cannot be more than one God for eternity, infinity, omnipresence, etc., cannot apply to more than one such being. Two such things would limit and exclude each other and thus render impossible the being of God. God makes himself known in the Scriptures as Father, Son and Holy Spirit, three separate personalities, three persons in one godhead, but not three gods. It is trinity and not tritheism (Deut 6.4; 1 Kgs 8.60; Isa 44.6; Mk 12.29; Jn 10.30; 1 Cor 8.4; Eph 4.6).

God the Creator. Creator of the heavens and the earth (Gen 1.1; Ex 20.11; Ps 8.3, 19.1; Jn 1.3; Acts 14.15; Rom 11.36; Heb 1.2). Creator of man (Gen 1.26; 5.1; Ex 4.11; Job 10.8-12; Ps 33.15; Ecc 12.1; Isa 43.1; Acts 17.25-29; 1 Cor 15.38).

Omnipotence. Unlimited in might and power (Gen 1.1,3; 18.14; Deut 32.39; Ps 66.3; Isa 40.12; Dan 4.35; Mt 19.26; Rom 1.20).

Omniscience. The all-knowing God, infinite in understanding as in power, and as in the case of his eternity and all other perfections, there can be no advance or progression in knowledge. (Job 37.16; Ps 33.13, 119.168; Jer 23.24; Mt 10.29; Acts 1.24, 15.18).

Omnipresence. His presence as his power extends over all his works (Job 34.21,22; Ps 139.7-12; Isa 66.1; Acts 17.27).

Immutability. God is no more subject to change than to any other limitation (Ps 33.11; Isa 46.10; Mal 3.6; Heb 1.12, 6.17,18; Jas 1.17).

Wisdom. (Job 36.5; Ps 104.24; Isa 28.29; Rom 16.27; 1 Tim 1.17).

Holiness. God is as essentially and infinitely holy as he is essentially and infinitely omnipotent, and requires holiness of the beings made in his image (Lev 19.2; Josh 24.19; 1 Sam 2.2; Job 36.2,3; Ps 89.35: Isa 5.16, 6.3; Hos 11.9, 1 Pet 1.15).

Justice. In the Scriptures justice and righteousness are used synonymously. In the being of God it is a necessary outflow from his holiness, the manifestation of that holiness in the moral government of the world. He is perfectly just as the righteous governor of the world, and his perfect righteousness appears in the penalties pronounced and rewards bestowed (Gen 18.25; Deut 10.17; Job 8.3,20; Ps 9.8, 119.142; Jer 11.20; Dan 9.7; Rom 2.11; Rev 15.3).

Mercy. The divine goodness and compassion exercised toward the guilty and wretched in harmony with truth and justice, the ministry of love for the relief of those unworthy of it (Ex 34.7; Deut 4.31, Ps 51.1, 117.2; Isa 55.7; Jer 3.12; Lk 1.50; 6.36; Eph 2.4; Titus 3.5; Heb 4.16).

Faithfulness. This divine attribute is noted especially in the Psalms. By it we are assured that God will fulfill his promises. As regards temporal necessities (Ps 84.11; Isa 33.16; 1 Tim 4.8). Support in temptation and persecution (Isa 41.10; 1 Cor 10.13; 1 Pet 4.12,13). In afflictions (Heb 12.4-12). Guidance in trouble (2 Chr 32.22; Ps 32.8).

Power to persevere (Jer 32.40). Spiritual blessings and final glory (1 Cor 1.9; Jn 2.25).

Love. Our conceptions of God must be derived from the revelation of himself in his Word, and in that revelation he declares this attribute of love. Not only so, but it is the only attribute by which his being as such is defined—"God is love." In both the Old and New Testaments God's gracious love to men is so strongly and frequently declared it would take considerable space to set down the passages (Ex 34.5; Isa 63.9; Jer 31.3; Jn 3.16; 1 Jn 4.10). The highest expression of divine love is in redemption—God in Christ reconciling the world unto himself (Rom 5.8, 8.32-39; 1 Jn 4.9,10).

The Triune God—Father, Son, Holy Spirit. The Scriptures set forth the Godhead in this distinction of persons with absolute unity of essence. At the beginning of our Lord's ministry the three persons are exhibited at his baptism, the Holy Spirit as a dove resting upon him, the Father speaking acknowledging the Son. In the formula of baptism the doctrine of trinity is established by the resurrected Lord (Mt 28.19).

1. *The Father is God.* (Mt 11.25; Jn 6.27, 8.41; Rom 15.6; 1 Cor 8.6; Ep 4.6; Jas 1.27).

2. *The Son is God.* (Jn 1.1,18, 20.28; Rom 9.5; Phil 2.6; Col 2.9; Heb 1.8; 2 Pet 1.1).

3. *The Spirit is God* (Acts 5.3,4; 1 Cor 2.10,11; Eph 2.22).

4. *The distinctiness of the three from one another* (Jn 15.26; 16.13,14; 17.1-8, 18-23).

GOLIATH A Philistine giant of the city of Gath. For forty days he defied the army of Israel (1 Sam 17). Estimating a cubit as eighteen inches he was over nine feet tall, and over ten feet if the cubit is reckoned as twenty-one inches. He was challenged by David, and in the valley of Terebinth he was slain by a stone from David's sling.

GRAVEN IMAGE. An image made by a sharp instrument as distinguished from one made in a mould. Stone, wood, and metal were used (Isa 30.22, 44.15,17, 45.20). They were made by the Canaanites before the land was taken by the Israelites (Deut 7.5, 12.3). The sin of making them was constantly impressed upon the Jews (Ex 20.4; Deut 5.8, 27.15; Isa 44.9; Jer 51.17).

H

HAGAR. Sarah's Egyptian bondwoman (Gen 16.1). She bore Abraham a son, Ishmael, after the patriarch decided to wait no longer for God's promise of an heir to be fulfilled through his 76-year-old wife, Sarah. When Sarah bore Isaac, Ishmael mocked the boy with the result that Hagar and Ishmael were expelled from Abraham's house into the wilderness.

HAM. The youngest son of Noah, born when Noah was five hundred years old (Gen 5.32, 6.10, 9.18). He and his two brothers survived the flood with Noah. After Ham saw his father naked, Noah cursed Ham's son, Canaan, to a life of continual servitude to his brothers (Gen 9.22-27). Ham was a founder of one of the three great families that repeopled the earth after the flood (Gen 10.1,6-20).

HAMAN. He was a high official in the court of King Ahasuerus. His intrigue against the Jews was exposed by Esther (Esth 7-9).

HANNAH. One of the two wives of Elkanah; the mother of Samuel. She was especially favored by her husband which aroused the hostility of the other wife who subjected her to annoyances. Hannah was childless, but vowed that if she became the mother of a son, she would dedicate him to the Lord's service. Samuel was born and Hannah kept her vow (1 Sam 1.1-28). Her triumphant song (1 Sam 2.1-10) may have been in the mind of Mary (Lk 1.26-55).

HARAN. A city of Mesopotamia in which Abraham settled after leaving Ur. He remained there until after the death of his father, Terah, and then he started for Canaan. The city was a commercial center. Jacob lived in Haran for a time (Gen 28.10, 29.4).

HEART. The word in the Scriptures has a wide significa-
tion. *First,* the physical heart the center of bodily life (Ps
40.8,10,12), and the things that contribute to its health
and strength (Judg 19.5; Acts 14.17). *Second,* the higher
rational, spiritual activities. The seat of the affections and
emotions as joy (Isa 65.14); fear (Deut 28.28; Ps 143.4);
hatred (Lev 19.17); love (1 Tim 1.5). *Third,* as expressive
of moral characteristics and conditions. The hardening of
the heart (Isa 6.10, 63.17; Jer 16.12; 2 Cor 3.15); the seat of
passions (Mk 4.15; Rom 1.24); for the moral government
of life God's law is written in the heart (Isa 51.7; Jer 31.33;
Rom 2.15; Heb 10.22). *Fourth,* the deeper spiritual life.
The dwelling place of Christ (Eph 3.17) and of the Holy
Spirit (2 Cor 1.22); where the love of God is felt (Rom
5.5); and his peace is realized (Col 3.15); where we enjoy
the deeper communion with God (Eph 5.19).

HEAVEN, THE HEAVENS. 1. The region about the
earth—the heavens and the earth (Gen 1.1), comprising
the universe (Gen 14.19; Jer 23.24). 2. The place of God's
presence from whence Christ came and to which he returned (Ps 80.14; Isa 66.1; Mt 5.16,45,48; Jn 3.13; Acts
1.11). It is from here he will come in his return to the earth
(Mt 24.30; Rom 8.33,34; 1 Thess 4.16; Heb 6.20). Heaven
is the future home of the redeemed (Eph 3.15; 1 Pet 1.4;
Rev 19.1-4).

HEBREW. 1. A designation first applied to Abraham, a
descendant of Eber (Gen 14.13). It was applied by foreigners to the Israelites (Gen 39.14,17, 41.12; Ex 1.16; 1
Sam 4.6,9) and the Israelites used the word in regard to
themselves (Gen 40.15; Ex 1.19). In the New Testament it
is used to describe those whose speech was Aramaic to
distinguish them from Greek-speaking Jews (Acts 6.1).
Paul called himself a Hebrew of the Hebrews, indicating
that his parents were of Hebrew stock (Phil 3.5). 2. Hebrew was the language of the Israelites. It is a Semitic
language consisting of twenty-two consonants and reads
from right to left. The Old Testament, with the exception

of a few portions written during the Exile and the Restoration, was written in Hebrew.

HEBRON. A town in the hill country of Judah, the oldest town of Palestine and one of the oldest in the world. It is about twenty miles from Beer-sheba and the same distance from Jerusalem. For a long time it was the residence of Abraham (Gen 13.18) and here Sarah was buried (Gen 23.17-20). Isaac and Jacob also lived here (Gen 35.27) and David made it his capital until the taking of Jerusalem (2 Sam 2.1-4, 5.5; 1 Kgs 2.11).

HEIR. Hebrew law relative to inheritance was simple. The property was divided between the sons of legitimate wife. The sons of a concubine did not inherit. Ishmael, the son of Hagar, the bondwoman, could not inherit because of Abraham's other son, Isaac, the son of Sarah, the free woman (Gen 21.10). The birthright falling to the eldest son secured for him a double portion of the property (Deut 21.15-17). If a man died childless the brothers inherited and if he had no brethren, the property went to his father's brethren (Num 27.9-11).

HERMON. A mountain on the northern boundary of the territory taken by the Israelites from the Amorites (Deut 3.8; Josh 11.3,17, 12.1,5). It rises 10,000 feet above the sea and is visible from most parts of Palestine. The Jordan river rises here. Hermon was doubtless the high mountain on which Christ was transfigured (Mk 9.2).

HEROD. The name of a number of Palestinian rulers. The most famous was Herod the Great, king of Judaea (37-4 B.C.). He was jealous of his power and killed many, even his sons, because he feared they would take his throne. When he heard that the King of the Jews had been born he ordered the death of all infants, so that Jesus might be destroyed (Mt 2.16). He was succeeded by his three sons, Archelaus, Herod Antipas, and Philip.

HERODIAS. Granddaughter of Herod the Great and sister of King Herod Agrippa. Herodias deserted her first husband, Herod Philip, and married Herod Antipas,

Philip's half-brother. Antipas divorced his first wife and when John the Baptist denounced this, he was imprisoned. Herodias was the mother of the dancer, Salome, who asked for and received the head of John the Baptist (Mt 14.3-12; Mk 6.17.29; Lk 3.19,20).

HEZEKIAH. King of Judah, son of Ahaz. Unlike his godless father, he was a man of outstanding piety in his service of Jehovah. He reorganized the temple service and celebrated the Passover to which he invited the tribes of Israel (2 Chr 29.1-30.13). He brought about a revival of religion and worked earnestly to drive out idolatry. He was greatly assisted by the prophet, Isaiah.

HOLY. The basic meaning which is that which is set apart for holy purposes. Things which in themselves were ordinary, such as utensils, became sacred, or holy when devoted to the service of the sanctuary. The same was true of those separated from the body of the people for the sacred office of the priesthood. Certain seasons and days were also holy (Ex 20.8; 31.10; Lev 21.7; Neh 8.9). Holiness is ascribed to God, since he is apart from and above every being in his infinite perfections and attributes. (1 Sam 2.2; Isa 6.3; Rev 4.8).

HOLY SPIRIT. He is the third person of the Trinity, thus not simply a divine energy or influence proceeding from God. As a person, he possesses intelligence, self-consciousness and self-determination. His personality is explicitly described (Mt 3.16,17; 28.19; Jn 14.16,17, 15.26). Personal pronouns used of him (Jn 16.13,14; Acts 13.2). His personal freedom (1 Cor 2.10, 12.11). He is distinctly addressed as God and designations are used that belong only to God (Acts 5.3,4; 2 Cor 3.17,18; Heb 10.15). Having the divine attributes of eternity, knowledge, sovereignty (1 Cor 2.11, 12.11; Heb 9.14). In his relation to Father and Son he is the same as they in divine substance, in power and glory. He proceeds from the Father and Son and in this relation is subordinate (not inferior) to them as they operate through him (Jn 15.26, 16.13; Phil 1.19).

40

HORN. The Israelites had many uses for the horns of animals. They made them into trumpets (Josh 6.13), and they used them as containers for oil (1 Sam 16.1,13). The horn was also a symbol of power (Ps 132.17; Jer 48.25) and of the monarchy (Dan 7.8,11,21; Zech 1.18,19). The corners of the altar for burnt offerings resembled horns (Ex 29.12; Lev 4.7).

HOST. A large body of things or people, such as an army. It is also used to designate the owner of a house at which one might stay (Rom 16.23). The stars are described as the "host of heaven" (Deut 4.19; 2 Kgs 23.5). The word also denotes all the beings of heaven, hence the angels were a heavenly host (1 Kgs 22.19; Ps 148.2; Lk 2.13).

HOUSE. The houses of the common people consisted ordinarily of one story and often of a single room. In Palestine brick, lime, and sandstone were used, while only the houses of the rich were made of hewn stone (1 Kgs 7.9; Isa 9.10). Houses of the more prosperous classes were built around a courtyard having a well (2 Sam 17.18). The second story contained the upper room or chamber (1 Kgs 17.19; 2 Kgs 4.10; Mk 14.15; Acts 1.13, 9.37). The roof surrounded by a low wall was flat for storing things (Josh 2.6), for social intercourse (1 Sam 9.25,26) and for religious purposes (2 Kgs 23.12; Acts 10.9). The roof could be reached by an outside stairway (Mt 24.17).

I

IDOLATRY. The worship of a god supposed to live within an idol, or the worship of the idol itself. This practices goes back to an early period in human history. In Babylon, prior to Abraham's time, idols were worshipped (Josh 24.2). The first reference to idolatry among the Hebrews is in the account of Rachel's theft of the images of Laban's gods (Gen 31.30,32-35). After they arrived in Canaan the Israelites were divinely commanded to destroy the idols of the Canaanites (Num 33.52; Deut 7.5, 29.17).

When the ten tribes revolted and formed the kingdom of Israel, Jeroboam set up images by which to worship Jehovah. Soon the idols came to represent other divinities and Jehovah was forsaken. Idolatry was encouraged by such kings as Ahab and Manasseh (2 Kgs 16.31-33; 2 Kgs 21.2-7).

IMMANUEL. The symbolic name of the child whose birth Isaiah promised as a sign of deliverance and safety to King Ahaz (Isa 7.14). The name is repeated in Isa 8.8. This prophesy was made at a time of national crisis (735 B.C.) when the kingdom of Ahaz was threatened with defeat by the combined armies of Syria and Ephraim. In addition to its immediate significance as a sign to Ahaz, it has always been regarded as a forewarning of the Messiah. This prophecy was fulfilled in the birth of Christ (Mt 1.23).

IMMORTALITY. The doctrine of continued existence after the death of the body. One distinguishing difference between the Pharisees and Sadducees was that the former believed in a resurrection and immortality while the latter denied both (Lk 20.27-38). The New Testament teaches that the righteous will be rewarded and the wicked punished after death (Mt 13.37-43; Jn 6.47-58, 14.1,2; 1 Cor 15.19-58; Gal 6.7,8; 1 Thess 4.13-18; Rev 14.13, 20.12-15).

INCARNATION. By this doctrine is taught that Christ, the son of God, became man, having the body and nature of human beings. That in one person were united two natures, divine and human. In his First Epistle John refuted the false teaching that denied that Jesus came in the flesh.

INCENSE. A fragrant substance burned in the religious services of the Israelites (Ex 25.6, 35.8, 28). Frankincense and other aromatic substances gave forth perfume by burning. The high priest burned incense each morning (Ex 30.1-9).

ISAAC. The son and heir of Abraham and Sarah who was born in Beer-sheba when his father was about one hundred years old and his mother about ninety (Gen 17.17; 21.2-3, 22.1,2). The parents were amazed to learn that Isaac would be born to them (Gen 18.9-15). Isaac had reached young manhood (Gen 22.6) when his father was commanded to offer him as a burnt offering. When the Lord was convinced that Abraham passed this test of faith, he spared Isaac's life (Gen 22.12). When forty years old he married Rebekah, sister of Laban (Gen 25.20,26). Two sons were born to them, Esau and Jacob (Gen 27-28).

ISHMAEL. The son of Abraham by Hagar, Sarah's Egyptian maid. At his birth Abraham was eighty-six years old (Gen 16.3,15). Ishmael was about fourteen years of age when Isaac was born, the child of promise and heir to the covenant promises (Gen 21.5). Paul makes use of the allegory relative to the mocking of Isaac by Ishmael (Gal 4.22-31). For this Ishmael and his mother were expelled from the home of Abraham and in their distress in the wilderness were divinely provided for.

ISRAEL. 1. The name of Jacob. His name was changed the night he spent at Peniel on his way to Canaan from Mesopotamia. It marked a turning point in his life (Gen. 32.22-30). 2. The covenant people, descendants of Jacob. Dating from the change of his name, the people were called "Israelites" (Gen 32.32). The name was often used during the period in the wilderness (Ex 32.4; Deut 4.1, 27.9). 3. The designation of the northern kingdom after the disruption of the United Kingdom. Division took place when the already rebellious northern tribes were confronted with the fact that Rehoboam, Solomon's son and successor, would not reduce the taxes and other burdens imposed by Solomon (1 Kgs 12.9-17). The northern kingdom set up its own religious centers which eventually became centers of idol worship, particularly of Baal. Idolatry was especially strong during the reign of Ahab (1 Kgs 16.30-33). Elijah labored in vain to end the idolatry. The kingdom of Israel ended with the fall of Samaria (721 B.C.) at which time many of the people were carried away to Assyria (2 Kgs 17.3-6).

ISSACHAR. 1. The ninth son of Jacob by his first wife, Leah (Gen 30.17,18, 35.23). 2. Tribe of Issachar. The territory of Issachar was south of Zebulun and Naphtali; south of it lay Manasseh and its eastern boundary was the Jordan.

J

JACOB. The twin-brother of Esau and the son of Isaac and Rebekah. Jacob was the favorite of his mother, Esau of his father. In his youth he tricked Esau into giving up his birthright and his father's blessing. Jacob then fled Esau's wrath to Haran when he lived in the home of Laban. He married Laban's daughters, Leah and Rachel. The latter, his favorite, gave birth to Joseph, his favored son. Later he returned, had a reconciliation with Esau, and settled in Canaan. On the return trip he changed his name to Israel (Gen 25-49).

JAIRUS. A ruler of the synagoge, probably at Capernaum (Mk 5.22,23; Lk 8.41). His daughter was raised from the dead by Jesus (Mk 5.35-43; Lk 8.49-56).

JAMES. 1. James the son of Zebedee and brother of John (Mt 4.21, 17.1; Mk 3.17). He and John were partners of Peter and Andrew in the fishing business (Lk 5.10). He and John were two of the first four apostles called by Jesus (Mt 4.21; Mk 1.19). His mother, Salome, was the sister of Mary, mother of Jesus. James is always mentioned in connection with John, and is spoken first from which it is inferred he was older than John (Mt 10.2; Mk 5.37; Lk 5.10). James was the first of the apostles to die for his Lord in the persecution of Herod (Acts 12.2). 2. James was the son of Alphaeus. He was one of the apostles (Mt 10.3; Mk 3.18; Lk 6.15; Acts 1.13). He was called James the Less, either on account of his stature or because he was younger than James, the brother of John (Mk 16.1). 3. James, the Lord's brother. That James and his sisters were the children of Joseph and Mary the mother of Jesus is the most natural interpretation of Mt 13.55; Mk 6.3. This James was not an apostle (Mt 10.2-4) and was not a believer in the Messiahship of Jesus (Jn 7.5) until after the resurrection (Acts 1.13,14). Then he headed the Church in Jerusalem.

JEHOSHAPHAT. Son and successor of Asa and one of the better kings of Judah. Conjointly with Asa, then alone, he reigned 25 years (1 Kgs 22.41,42; 2 Chr 17.1). He honored Jehovah, carried forward the reforms of Asa, and commissioned the Levites to instruct the people in the law (2 Chr 17.7-9). He also brought an end to the conflicts between Israel and Judah.

JEREMIAH. The great prophet who worked at the time of the fall of Judah. He was the son of Hilkiah (Jer 1.1). Jeremiah began his work in the thirteenth year of the reign of King Josiah (627 B.C.), continued through the declining years of the kingdom, and for some time after its fall (586 B.C.).

JEROBOAM. The founder of the northern kingdom of Israel. His father was an official under Solomon (1 Kgs 11.26) and Jeroboam, because of his ability, was made overseer of a part of Solomon's building operations at Jerusalem (1 Kgs 11.27,28). Jeroboam represented the ten tribes in demanding that the tax burdens be lightened. Rehoboam's foolish reply brought about the disruption and, with Jeroboam as their leader, ten tribes revolted (1 Kgs 12).

JERUSALEM. An ancient city, which was known as Salem in the time of Abraham (Gen 14.18, Ps 76.2), and called Jebus at the time of its occupation by the Jebusites (Judg 19.10,11). In the time of Joshua the name Jerusalem began to be used and by the time it was captured by David, it was the common name for the city. Jerusalem is about fifteen miles from the Jordan River, situated in the Judean highlands at an elevation of about 2,500 feet. Jerusalem has an almost unbroken history of over four thousand years. It was mentioned in records of the conquering

Pharaohs. There are still in existence letters written in the fourteenth century B.C. by its Hittite ruler. Its capture by David around 1000 B.C. laid the basis for its subsequent religious and political importance. After Solomon built the Temple, the city became the religious center of Israel.

JESSE. Son of Obed, father of David, and grandson of Ruth and Boaz. He was descended from Nahshon who in the days of Moses was chief of the tribe of Judah (Ruth 4.18-22). David was the youngest of the eight sons of Jesse (1 Sam 17.12-14).

JESUS CHRIST. 1. **Name.** The name Jesus, announced by the angel as that divinely selected for Mary's son (Mt 1.21; Lk 1.31-33), signifies *the Lord is salvation.* The word Christ (the anointed one) is essentially an official title borne by Jesus as the Messiah (Jn 1.41) and as the Son of the living God (Mt 16.16).

2. **Date.** Jesus was born in the year 4 (some say late 5) B.C. The Roman abbot who (prior to A.D. 550) devised the Christian calendar fixed the year 1, the year intended for Christ's birth, too late.

3. **Early life.** The events and circumstances connected with the birth of Jesus (Mt 1,2; Lk 1.26-35, 2.1-39) are well-known. The genealogy of the family is traced by Matthew to Abraham and by Luke to Adam.

4. **His baptism.** John the Baptist, probably in the summer of A.D. 26, began to proclam the approach of the day of the Lord. John called upon individuals and nation to repent and be baptized. Among the Galilaeans who came to the region of the lower Jordan to be baptized was Jesus. As an individual Jesus had no need of baptism but submitting to it, he identified himself with men as their Redeemer. It was at his baptism that he heard the heavenly voice declaring him to be the beloved son in whom God was well pleased (Mt 3.1-17; Mk 1.10,11).

5. **His temptation.** After the baptism, Jesus was led by the Spirit into the wilderness to be tempted (Mt 4.1-11; Lk 4.1-13).

6. **Early Judean ministry.** After certain rather informal opening events which included the calling of some disciples and the miracle at Cana (Jn 1.35-47, 2.1-11), Jesus began his work in Judea, making occasional visits to Galilee (Jn 4.3). Among the recorded events of this period were the cleansing of the Temple, the conversations with Nicodemus, and with the woman at the well (Jn 2.13-17, 3.1-21, 4.3-26).

7. **The early or main Galilaean ministry.** The fame which Jesus had achieved in Judea preceded him into Galilee (Jn 4.43-45). The synagogue at Nazareth rejected him at the outset (Lk 4.16-30) but the people generally gave him a tumultuous welcome. He declared that the Spirit of the Lord was upon him and that he was anointed to preach the gospel to the poor (Lk 4.18-21). He moved his residence from Nazareth to Capernaum; called additional disciples; and performed many miracles of healing (Mt 4.13, 18-22, 9.2-6,9; Jn 4.46-54). Doctrine was presented through the Sermon on the Mount (Mt 5.1-7.29), various discourses and parables (Mt 13.1-53).

8. **The later Galilaean ministry in northern Galilee and beyond.** He elicited from Peter his great confession, he foretold his death and resurrection, and was manifested to certain disciples in the transfiguration (Mt 16.13-28, 17.1-13).

9. **The Perean ministry.** At this time he uttered many of his most famous parables (Lk 10.30-37, 15-16.1-12, 19-31). He delivered discourses on prayer, on the coming of the kingdom, and against the Pharisees (Lk 11.1-13,37-54, 17.20-37).

10. **Passion Week.** Six days before the Passover Jesus went to Bethany where Mary anointed his head with precious ointment (Jn 12.1-8). On the next day he made his triumphal entry into Jerusalem (Mt. 21.1-11; Jn 12.12-19), then returned to Bethany, probably to the house of Mary, Martha, and Lazarus. On Monday he entered Jerusalem, cleansed the Temple and cursed a barren fig tree

which by the following day had withered away (Mt 11.11-26). On Tuesday he went again to Jerusalem where his authority was challenged by the religious leaders (Mt 21.23-27). He pronounced woes against the scribes and Pharisees but commended the poor widow who cast two mites into the Temple treasury (Mt 23; Mk 12.41-44). He delivered a lengthy discourse on the destruction of the Temple, the end of the world, and the last judgment (Mt 24-25.31-46). It was on this day that Judas Iscariot conspired to betray him (Mt. 26.3,14-16). On Wednesday he remained in retirement at Bethany. On Thursday he instituted the Last Supper, delivered farewell discourses (Mt 26.17-30; Jn 13.1-17.26). On Friday he underwent the agony in Gethsemane, was betrayed by Judas, and was arrested (Lk 22.39-54; Jn 18.1-28). His trial was first before the Jewish authorities, then before Pilate. Pilate found no fault in him but, in order to pacify the Jews who clamored for his death, turned him over to them for execution (Jn 18.29-19.22).

11. **His death, burial and resurrection.** See CRUCIFIXION. When death came to Jesus on the cross, the crowd had dispersed but a few faithful followers remained. Joseph of Arimathaea, a secret disciple of Jesus and member of the Sanhedrin and Nicodemus, another secret disciple and a member of the Sanhedrin, also came, bringing myrrh and aloes. The little group bound the body with linen cloths and spices, then placed it in a new, rock-hewn tomb (Mt 27.26-66, 28; Mk 15.16-47, 16; Lk 23.32-56, 24; Jn 19.23-21.25). Despite the huge stone which had been rolled against the door of the tomb and the watch which had been placed on guard, Jesus rose on the third day (Mt 28.1-7).

JEZEBEL. A Phoenician princess (1 Kgs 16.31). She became the wife of Ahab, king of Israel, and became the power behind the throne. She was a zealous worshipper of Baal and established that idolatry in Israel (1 Kgs 16.32,33). She killed the prophets of Jehovah (1 Kgs 18.4-

13) and by false judicial action had Naboth slain (1 Kgs 21.16-22). The divine judgment that she would be devoured by dogs was fulfilled when Jehu put to death the house of Ahab (2 Kgs 9.7-10, 30-37).

JOAB. He was a companion of David in his exile and commander-in-chief of his troops throughout his reign. Joab was an efficient general who was also independent in his attitude toward King David. Occasionally he disobeyed David's instruction, as in the case of the slaying of Abner and Absalom (2 Sam 3.22-39, 18.10-15).

JOHN. 1. *John the Baptist.* The son of Zacharias. His mother Elisabeth, was a descendant of Aaron (Lk 1.5) and a cousin of the Virgin Mary. When the angel informed Zacharius that a son was to be born to them, he instructed him to name him John (Lk 1.8-17). John's early years were spent in seclusion in the wilderness, and there, near the Jordan, he began his preaching as the forerunner of Jesus (Mt 3.1-3). His preaching was designed to prepare the hearts of the people for the acceptance of the Christ about to appear. When our Lord at baptism began his public ministry, it was John who baptized him (Mt 3.13-17). John denounced Herod Antipas for taking as wife Herodias, the wife of his half-brother Philip and was imprisoned by Herod (Lk 3.19,20). Later at the solicitation of Herodias he was beheaded (Mt 14.1-12). 2. *John the Apostle.* He and James were sons of Zebedee. It is believed their mother was Salome. They were fishermen on the Sea of Galilee in partnership with Peter (Lk 5.10). After Pentecost he remained in Jerusalem during the persecutions of the early Christian and was active with Peter in missionary labors (Acts 3.1, 15.6; Gal 2-9).

JONATHAN. Saul's eldest son. His father gave him the command of 1000 men at Geba at which point he defeated the Philistine garrison (1 Sam 13.3). The friendship of David and Jonathan began when David slew Goliath and it continued in the face of Saul's persecution of David (1 Sam 18.1-4). He acted in behalf of David (1 Sam 20.1-42), and they entered into "a covenant before the Lord" (1 Sam 23.15-18). We hear nothing more of him until Saul's last battle at Gilboa when Jonathan and his two brothers were slain by the Philistines and Saul took his own life (1 Sam 31.1,11-13; 1 Chr 10.2,8-12). David deeply lamented his death (2 Sam 1.17-27) and cared for Jonathan's crippled son, Mephibosheth (2 Sam 4.4).

JORDAN. The famous river of Palestine. At Lake Huleh it is only a few feet above sea level. From this marshy region it continues to the Sea of Galilee where it is almost 700 feet below the level of the Mediterranean. Ninety miles farther south, where it empties into the Dead Sea, the Jordan reaches a depth of 1,292 feet below sea level. In its course the river receives two tributaries from the east, the Yarmuk and the Jabbok.

JOSEPH. 1. *The eleventh son of Jacob.* Because of jealousy, his brothers caused him to be sold as a slave and carried into Egypt (Gen 30.22-24, 37.2-36). Because he was able to interpret Pharaoh's dream, he was placed in a high position in Egypt and made responsible for preparing the country against the famine. Later after he met his brothers, he brought his family to Egypt so that they could weather the famine. In his high position Joseph was able to preserve many Israelites from the famine (Gen 39.1-48.22). He lived in Egypt until his death at the age of one hundred and ten (Gen 50.26). 2. *The husband of Mary*, the mother of Jesus (Mt 1.16; Lk 3.23). When Augustus issued his decree that all should be enrolled, or taxed, Joseph and Mary went to Bethlehem. At that time Jesus was born (Mic 5.2; Lk 2.4, 16). After the death of Herod, they returned to Nazareth from Egypt (Mt 2.22,23). He was a carpenter (Mt 13.55). At the beginning of our Lord's work Joseph was evidently alive (Mt 13.55) but probably died prior to the crucifixion since, on the cross, Jesus committed his mother to the care of John (Jn 19.26,27). 3. *Joseph of Arimathaea.* He was a member of the Sanhedrin and, like Nicodemus, was a secret disciple of Jesus. He took a positive stand regarding his Lord and had the body placed in a new tomb which belonged to him (Mt 27.58-60; Mk 15.43-46).

JOSHUA. The son of Nun. His name was changed by Moses from Oshea to Joshua (Num 13.8,16). He was the commander of the Israelites in their first battle and defeated the Amalekites at Rephidim (Ex 17.8-16). He was with Moses on Sinai (Ex 24.13, 32.17). He was the representative of Ephraim when the twelve spies were sent to Canaan and he and Caleb strove to persuade the people to go and occupy the land (Num 13.8, 14.6-9). The Lord rewarded their loyalty, allowing them to settle in the land. At the end of the wandering, by divine direction, Moses placed Joshua before the high priest and publicly ordained him as his successor (Num 27.18-23; Deut 1.38, 31.14,23). His leadership of Israel is recorded in the book that bears his name.

JUDAH. 1. The fourth son of Jacob. His mother was Leah, Jacob's first wife. His two sons, Er and Onan, by his Canaanitish wife, were slain for their sinfulness by divine judgment (Gen 38:1-10). In Jacob's dying prophetical vision Judah was selected as the tribe of the Messiah (Gen 49:10). 2. The tribe occupied the large part of southern Palestine. Its western boundary was the Mediterranean, and the eastern the Dead Sea. From north to south the length of its territory was about fifty miles. In 931 B.C., occurred the division of the Kingdom. Ten of the tribes revolted under Jeroboam and formed the kingdom of Israel which existed from 931 to 722 B.C., while Judah continued until 586 B.C.

JUDAS. 1. Judas Iscariot. His motive in following Jesus would seem to be of a mercenary nature expecting to gain a worldly advantage in the establishment of the kingdom. He had charge of the funds of the band, and John declared he was a thief (Jn 12.6). He bargained with the chief priests to betray Jesus, the compensation being a little less than $30; what was ordinarily paid for a slave. At the Last

Supper he was declared by our Lord to be the traitor and that night earned his fee in the garden of Gethsemane (Mt 26.47-50). When he awoke to the enormity of his guilt, he confessed to the chief priests the sinfulness of his act and returned the money. His last act was to hang himself (Ma 27.3-5; Acts 1.18). 2. An apostle, distinguished from Judas Iscariot (Jn 14.22). He was called Thaddaeus (Mt 10.3; Mk 3.18), as well as Lebbaeus.

JUDGE. A civil magistrate invested with authority to hear and decide disputes. Moses originally acted as the only judge in Israel (Ex 18.13-26). When the monarchy was established, the king became the supreme judge in civil affairs (2 Sam 15.2; 1 Kgs 3.9,28, 7.7).

JUSTIFICATION. This doctrine sets forth the judicial act of God, by which sinners, meeting the divine terms, are released from condemnation and restored to divine favor. Justification denotes the change effected in man's relation to God. Justification is also to be distinguished from adoption, the latter, not a judicial act, but the act of God as Father, the sinner by grace being restored to God in a filial relationship (Rom 5.1,2, 8.29; 2 Cor 5.17,21; Gal 4.6; Eph 2.5).

K

KING. The head of a kingdom such as Pharaoh (Gen 12.15), Nebuchadnezzar and others, who exercised the chief rulership over a state. In the time of the judges the nations about Palestine were ruled by kings. The Israelites then demanded that a monarchy be established. This, however, did not abolish the theocracy. In Rev 19.16, Christ is called the King of kings.

KINGDOM. The universe is the kingdom of God over which he exercises rulership (Ps 22.28, 145.13; Mt 6.13). In Daniel's man-image, God will set up an everlasting kingdom (Dan 2.44). The kingdom of grace distinct from the kingdoms of the world is called the kingdom of heaven and the kingdom of God. Its character is illustrated by our Lord's parables (Mt 13.24,31,33,44; Mk 4.11,26; Lk 14.15).

KISS. In patriarchal times and later a kiss was a common form of salutation. Children were kissed by their parents (Gen 31.28,55, 48.10), children kissed parents (Gen 27.26,27; 1 Kgs 19.20), and brothers kissed each other (Gen 45.15; Ex 4.27), as did other relatives (Gen 29.11; Ruth 1.9). Between friends of the same sex it was the usual form of greeting (1 Sam 20.41; Acts 20.37). When a guest entered a house, it was customary for the one receiving to kiss the guest (Lk 7.45). Paul's injunction was to greet each other with a holy kiss (Rom 16.16; 2 Cor 13.12). There was nothing unusual about Judas kissing Jesus (Ps 2.12; Mt 26.49; Lk 22.47,48).

L

LABAN. He lived at Haran in Padan-aram (Gen 24.10,15, 28.5,10). Jacob stayed with him after fleeing the fury of Esau. Eventually Jacob married his two daughters, Leah and Rachel (Gen 29.16-28). On Mount Gilead Laban made a convenant with Jacob (Gen 29-31).

LAMB. Lambs were used both as food and as sacrificial offerings. A lamb was used as a burnt offering every morning and evening. Four were used on the Sabbath (Num 28.3,4,9). Seven lambs were offered on the first of the month and lambs were also sacrificed on the day of atonement and on all high feast days (Num 28.11,19,27, 29.2,8,13). Sacrificial lambs were generally male, and without blemish (Ex 12.5). The gentleness of the lamb has caused it to become a symbol of innocence and uncomplaining submissiveness. Christ is called the Lamb of God (Jn 1.29,36), also the Lamb (Rev 5.6,8).

LAVER. A basin for washing. The laver of the tabernacle was made of brass (copper) and placed between the tabernacle and altar. It rested upon a metal base, the base and laver being made of the mirrors of the women (Ex 38.8). Before serving at the altar or in the sanctuary, the priests washed their hands and feet in the laver which symbolized holiness in God's service (Ex 30.17-21; Lev 8.11).

LAW. The word *law* is the usual rendering of the Hebrew word *Torah,* instruction. The expression "the law" sometimes denotes the whole of the Old Testament (Jn 12.34, 15.25) but much more frequently is applied to the Pentateuch (Josh 1.8; Neh 8.2,3,14; Mt 5.17; Lk 16.16, Jn 1.17). The law of Moses, that which God revealed through Moses and recorded in the books of Moses (Ex 20.19-22; Mt 15.4), includes the legislation of Exodus, Leviticus, Numbers, Deuteronomy.

LAWYER. The professional interpreter of the law of Moses and not a legal practitioner in the present-day sense (Mt 22.35; Lk 10.25, 11.45-52, 14.3).

LAYING ON OF HANDS. The Levites were dedicated to divine service by having the Israelites lay their hands upon them (Num 8.5-20). Timothy was dedicated to the ministry when the hands of the presbytery were laid upon his head (1 Tim 4.14). The hands of the offerer were laid on the sacrificial animal (Lev 1.4, 16.21).

LAZARUS. 1. A resident of Bethany, the brother of Mary and Martha and the subject of Jesus' greatest miracle, resurrection from the dead (Jn 11.1-46). 2. The beggar in the story of the rich man and Lazarus (Lk 16.19-31).

LEAH. Laban's daughter who, by the trickery of Laban, became Jacob's first wife (Gen 29.16-35, 30.17-21).

LEAVEN. Unfermented dough used to make bread rise (Ex 13.7). The Jews were required to keep it from all offerings made by fire (Lev 2.11). It was allowed only when the offering was to be eaten (Lev 7.13). It was prohibited because it was emblematic of corruption. During the Passover week no leaven was allowed in the house. It was used figuratively to denote false doctrine (Mt 16.11) and impure conduct (1 Cor 5.6-8).

LEPER. One afflicted with leprosy. He was not permitted to mingle with others, and in approaching people he had to cry out the warning, "Unclean! unclean!" (Lev 13.45; Lk 17.12,13). The symptoms of this fearful disease are set forth in Lev 13.1-46. Beginning with a scab or bright spot, it would spread. The leper was required to come to the priest frequently who judged the stage of the disease and if it showed signs of departing, much cleansing and sacrificing was required (Lev 14.1-32).

LEGION. The main subdivision of the Roman army, the number running to six thousand men (Mt 26.53; Mk 5.9).

LEVITES. Descendants of Levi, son of Jacob. The Levites at Sinai remained true to Jehovah, and were chosen for religious services (Ex 32.26.29; Num 3.9,11-13,40,41, 8.16-18). At thirty years of age the Levites were eligible to full service in connection with the sanctuary (Num 4.3; 1 Chr 23.3-5), although they began to assist in these duties at the age of twenty (1 Chr 23.24,28-31).

LORD. The name of God (Gen 3.4-22). It is the Old Testament translation of the sacred name, YHWH. It was also a common noun meaning one in possession of authority (Gen 45.8; Josh 13.3). Christ was also called Lord (Lk 2.11; Jn 13.1; Acts 2:36).

LOT. He came with Abraham from Mesopotamia to Canaan (Gen 11.31, 12.5), went with him to Egypt, and returned to Canaan (Gen 13.1). When trouble arose over the matter of pasturage, they decided to separate. Lot was given the first selection as to district. He chose the Jordan valley and made Sodom his residence. When divine judgment fell upon Sodom, Lot and his family were saved from destruction (Gen 19:1-29).

LUKE. A friend and traveling companion of Paul (Col 4.14; 2 Tim 4.11; Phil 24) who wrote the third Gospel and Acts. A Greek, he was a doctor and is often referred to as the beloved physician. He joined Paul at Troas (Acts 16.10) and remained with him about nine years.

LYSTRA. Paul visited this city on his first journey. After he healed a lame man, the people insisted that he and Barnabas be worshipped as gods which Paul prevented. Later he was stoned (Acts 14.6-21; 2 Tim 3.11). It was here that Timothy lived (Acts 16.1,2).

M

MACEDONIA. A country north of Greece. It rose to world-wide power under Philip of Macedon (359-336 B.C.) and his celebrated son Alexander the Great (336-323 B.C.). Paul received a vision to preach in Macedonia (Acts 16.9, 20.1).

MAGICIAN. The magician claimed that he possessed supernatural powers that came through connections with evil spirits. The magicians of the Bible acquired considerable knowledge (Ex 7.11) and claimed to be able to interpret dreams (Gen 41.8, Dan 2.10).

MANASSEH. 1. The elder son of Joseph and brother of Ephraim (Gen 41.50,51, 48.8-21). 2. Tribe of Manasseh. A half of the tribe was settled east of the Jordan and the other half west of the Jordan in the central section, north of Ephraim (Num 32.33,42; Deut 3.13-15; Josh 13.29-33).

MANNA. The food of the Israelites during the time of their wandering, sent to them first in the wilderness of Sin (Ex 16.1-4,12; Ps 78.24, 105.40). It was white like coriander seed, having the taste of honey (Ex 16.31; Num 11.8). For each member of the family a little over five pints were gathered each day and on the sixth day double the quantity, as it was not sent on the Sabbath (Ex 16.22-30).

MARRIAGE. A divine institution, the condition of the propagation of the race (Gen 1.27,28). Monogamous, the union of one man and one woman (Gen 2.18-24; Mt 19.5; 1 Cor 6.16). A permanent relation dissolved by death (Rom 7.2,3). When the wedding day arrived the bride in white robes (Rev 19.8), adorned with jewels (Isa 61.10; Rev 21.2) and covered with a veil (Gen 24.65). The bridegroom in company with friends, attended by musicians went to the home of the bride (Judg 14.11; Isa 61.10; Mt 9.15), if at night torches were carried (Mt 25.7). The marriage relation is used figuratively to express the spiritual relation between Jehovah and his people (Isa 62-4,5; Hos 2.19; Mt 9.15; Jn 3.29; 2 Cor 11.2; Rev 19.7, 21.2,9, 22.17).

MARTHA Sister of Mary and Lazarus of Bethany (Jn 11.1,2). Jesus was a frequent guest at their home. Martha once complained to Jesus that Mary should do more housework but Jesus defended Mary's interest in things of a spiritual nature (Lk 10.38-42).

MARY. 1. *The Virgin Mary, mother of Jesus.* She lived in Nazareth and was betrothed to Joseph, a carpenter, a descendant of David (Lk 1.26,27). She was informed by the angel, Gabriel, that she would be the mother of the promised Messiah (Lk 1.32,33, 35). The "brethren of the Lord" were doubtless the children of Mary and Joseph. There were also sisters (Mk 6.3) so that Mary was the mother of a large family. 2. *Mary, the wife of Clopas or Cleophas* (Jn 19.25). They were the parents of James the Less, an apostle, and of Joses (Mt 27.56; Mk 15.40; Lk 24.10). Mary followed the body of Jesus to the tomb (Mt 27.61) and was there on the third day with spices (Mt 28.1; Mk 15.47, 16.1; Lk 24.10). 3. *Mary Magdalene.* A resident, doubtless, of Magdala, on the southwestern coast of the Sea of Galilee (Mt 27.56,61, 28.1, Mk 15.40,47; Lk 8.2, 24.10; Jn 19.25, 20.11-18). She was afflicted with seven demons which Jesus expelled (Mk 16.9, Lk 8.2). She was a devoted follower of her Lord (Lk 8.1-3) and was at the cross (Mt 27.56; Mk 15.40; Jn 19.25) and at the sepulchre on the third day (Mk 16.1). Mark states that Jesus, after his resurrection, appeared first to her (Mk 16.9). 4. *Mary of Bethany*, sister of Martha and Lazarus (Jn 11.1, 12.1). For the facts relative to the visit of Jesus see MARTHA. She was a woman of deep spiritual appreciations (Lk 10.38-42). 5. *Mary, mother of Mark.* She was a Christian woman, and it was at her house the disciples met for prayer at the time of the imprisonment of Peter by Herod Agrippa I (Acts 12.12). It is believed that the early Christians of Jerusalem made her house one of their meeting places.

MATTHEW A publican or taxgatherer who, before he was called by Jesus to discipleship, was called Levi, the son of Alphaneus. (Mt 9.9; Lk 5.27).

MEDITERRANEAN SEA. To the Hebrews this was the Great Sea (Num 34.6; Josh 15.47), also called the western sea (Deut 11.24; Joel 2.20). It lies between Africa and Europe and is about 2000 miles long.

MELCHIZEDEK. The king-priest of Salem (doubtless Jerusalem) (Gen 14.18). He is described as being without parents. But this probably means that his genealogy was not recorded (Heb 7.1-3). When he met Abraham, he refreshed him with bread and wine, received tithes from him, and blessed him (Gen 14.17-20). The endless priesthood of the Messiah, the Lord Jesus Christ is declared to be after the order of Melchizedek (Ps 110.4; Heb 7.15-17).

MERCY SEAT. The lid of the ark of the covenant, made of pure gold. Upon it were the two cherubim facing each other with their outstretched wings extending over the mercy seat. Between the cherubim the glory of God was exhibited (Ex 25.17-22, 30.6, Num 7.89). The mercy seat signified atonement (Ex 26.34; Heb 9.5).

MERIBAH. A place near Rephidim where the Israelites became angry at Moses because of the lack of water. Moses then struck a rock and water gushed forth (Ex 17.1-7; Num 20.1-13, 27.14; Deut 32.51).

MESOPOTAMIA. The Greek name for the country located between the Euphrates and Tigris rivers (Gen 24.7-10).

MESSIAH. The anticipated king and deliverer of the O.T. fulfilled by the coming of Jesus Christ. The term was originally applied to one anointed with holy oil, as high priest or king. Isaiah foretold the coming of a child, Immanuel, whose name would be the Lord's pledge of salvation for his people (Isa 7.14-17). The Messiah was next identified with a descendant of David and his reign was declared to be everlasting (Isa 9.6,7). Micah predicted that he would be born in Bethlehem (Mic 5.2). Many of the Psalms (as Ps 2) are Messianic. Jesus acknowledged himself to be the Christ or Messiah (Mk 14.61,62).

METHUSELAH. The son of Enoch of the line of Seth and an ancestor of Jesus (Gen 5.21-27). The oldest man in the Scriptures, he lived to be 969 years old.

MIDIANITES. A nomadic people of northwestern Arabia. They are represented as descendants of Abraham and Keturah. Joseph was carried to Egypt by Midianite merchants (Gen 37.28). Jethro, the father-in-law of Moses, was a Midianite (Ex 3.1).

MIRACLE. A sign, a special manifestation of God. They set forth God's character, and are used to accredit his messengers. Used only on specific and necessary occasions, for instance during such periods as the time of Moses and Joshua, of the divided kingdom, and of the Exile. Our Lord referred to his miracles in support of his divine claims, consequently more belong to this period than to all the others combined.

MIRIAM. Sister of Aaron and Moses (Ex 15.20, Num 26.59). When the Israelites passed through the Red Sea, she took a timbrel and sang a song of triumph (Ex 15.20, 21). In a spirit of jealousy, she and Aaron took a seditious attitude relative to the leadership of Moses, making the occasion of their murmuring Moses' marriage with a Cushite woman. Miriam was smitten with leprosy. Moses interceded for her and she was healed (Num 12.1-16; Deut 24.9).

MONEY CHANGER. One who exchanged foreign for native money or who changed money into different denominations. Jesus rebuked them and cast them from the Temple (Mt 21.12,13; Mk 11.15-17, Lk 19.45,46; Jn 2.13-16).

MOON. One of the celestial bodies. It was worshipped as a god by many ancient peoples including the Egyptians, Assyrians, and Babylonians. Some Hebrews worshipped the moon (Jer 19.13; Zeph 1.5) despite the fact that it was forbidden (Deut 17.3-5). The most famous temple to the moon god was in the city of Ur of the Chaldees. The moon served as a measure for marking off months and in regulating feasts (Gen 1.14; Ps 104.19).

MOSES. This great leader and lawgiver of the covenant people was the brother of Aaron, the head of the priestly family, and also the brother of Miriam. The first mention of him is in connection with the incident in the bulrushes of the Nile when as a baby he was found by Pharaoh's daughter (Ex 2.10). At the age of 40 he killed an Egyptian and as a result fled to the region of Horeb. There he lived with Jethro, priest of Midian, and later married his daughter, Zipporah, who bore him two sons (Ex 2.11-22, 18.1-4; Acts 7.23-29). After forty years, the Lord bid him to liberate his people from Egypt (Ex 3.1-10; Acts 7.30-36). He obeyed and henceforth, from the plagues of Egypt through the difficulties of the Exodus and forty years of wandering, to his death and burial on the mountains of Moab (Deut 34.1-7), his influence continually increased.

MOURNING. The Oriental expressed his grief in a very noticeable manner, by tearing his garments (2 Sam 13.31; Joel 2.13), putting on sackcloth, and sprinkling on his head dust or ashes (2 Sam 15.32; Joel 1.8), by removing from his person anything of an ornamental nature (2 Sam 14.2, 19.24; Mt 6.16-18). Professional mourners, mainly women, were sometimes employed (Jer 9.17,18; Mt 9.23; Acts 9.39). There was an extended period of mourning. They mourned for Aaron and Moses thirty days (Num 20.29; Deut 34.8) and for Saul seven days (1 Sam 31.13).

N

NABOTH. A man of Jezreel, owner of a vineyard that Ahab, king of Israel, wanted to buy. Jezebel, wife of

Ahab, had Naboth and his sons put to death (2 Kgs 9.26 and Ahab seized the vineyard. The judgment of God was pronounced against them (1 Kgs 21.1-24; 22.34-38; 2 Kgs 9.30-37).

NAPHTALI. 1. Son of Jacob by Bilhah, Rachel's maid. Rachel wrestled in prayer for a son, hence the name (Gen 30:8). 2. The tribe descended from the four sons of Naphtali (Gen 46:24; Nu. 26:48,49).

NAZARETH. A town on an elevation in Galilee, not mentioned in the Old Testament. It is about twenty miles southwest of Capernaum. It was the home of Joseph and Mary, and of Jesus until he entered upon his public ministry at the age of thirty (Mt 2.23; Lk 2.39, 4.16).

NAZARITE. The word is derived from the verb that denotes to separate and signifies that one, male or female, is especially consecrated to God. The Nazarite took a vow by which his life, for a certain time, would be devoted to the Lord. The Nazarite law was one of the legislations of Sinai by which he was forbidden to drink wine or strong drink, his hair must remain uncut, it being the product of his body that is devoted to God, and he had to keep himself ceremonially clean (Num 6.1-21; Deut 15.19).

NEBUCHADNEZZAR. Most famous of the Babylonian kings. In 625 B.C., his father founded the New Babylonian Empire which became one of the first of the world empires. Upon the death of his father, Nebuchadnezzar ascended the throne. In biblical history he is linked with three great prophets, Jeremiah, Ezekiel, Daniel. In 606 B.C., in the reign of Jehoiakim, he invaded Palestine, placed it under tribute (2 Kgs 24.1), and carried away some of the people, one of whom was Daniel. In 597 B.C., he returned and carried to Babylon the king, Jehoiachin, and many of the people, one of them Ezekiel.

NEHEMIAH. A Jewish statesman, patriot, and reformer of the period of the Exile. While at the Persian capital, Nehemiah requested permission of Artaxerxes, the king, to go to Jerusalem, because of reports reaching him concerning the poor state of affairs there. The permission was granted. His first task was to rebuild the wall of the city. This was completed in two months by the inhabitants (Neh 2.10-6.15). He then turned his attention to religious reform. He had the book of the law read publicly, the Feast of the Tabneracles observed, the new walls dedicated, and a covenant to observe all obligations signed (Neh 8-10).

NICODEMUS. He was a Pharisee and member of the Sanhedrin. Our Lord stated the nature, necessity, and agency of the new birth which comes by faith in Christ and regeneration by the Spirit (Jn 3.1-21; 7.50-52).

NILE. The one great river of Egypt (Isa 23.3). The land promised to Abraham for his posterity was from the river of Egypt to the river Euphrates (Gen 15.18). In connection with the sojourn of the Israelites in Egypt, the Nile is frequently mentioned. Its waters were turned to blood by the Lord when the Pharoah refused to allow Moses to lead the Israelites out of Egypt (Ex 7.20).

NOAH. He was divinely instructed to build an ark on which he, his family, and at least two of each kind of animal were to survive the flood planned by the Lord to rid the world of wickedness (Gen 6.14-8.19).

O

OATH. An oath was taken declaring a statement to be true, or to assure the keeping of a promise (Gen 21.23, 31.53; Gal 1.20; Heb 6.16). When God made his promise, he confirmed it by an oath (Heb 6.13-20).

OIL. Except for the once-mentioned oil of myrrh (Esth 2.12), all scriptural references to oil are to olive oil. This product was put to a variety of uses by the Hebrews. It was an article of food, serving the purpose of butter (1 Kgs 17.12,14), a cosmetic (Isa 61.3), a fuel for lamps (Ex 25.6, 27.20), and a healing agent (Is 1.6, Mk 6.13). It was also an ingredient of the meal offering (Lev 2.1,4-7). Oil was an important article of commerce (Ezek 27.17; Hos 12.1). The olives were beaten or shaken from the trees (Deut 24.20; Isa 17.6, 24.13), then subjected to pressure.

OLIVE. This tree was grown extensively in Palestine (Josh 24.13; Judg 15.5, 1 Sam 8.14). For its oil see OIL. Paul refers to the process of grafting a wild olive into the good or cultivated olive tree (Rom 11.17,24).

OLIVES, MOUNT OF. A place where olive trees grew. This hill, which consists of four peaks, is separated from Jerusalem by the Kidron valley and to its summit from Jerusalem was a Sabbath-day's journey (Acts 1.12). On the western slope is the garden of Gethsemane.

ONESIMUS. A slave of the Christian, Philemon of Colossae, who ran away from his master to Rome. There he met Paul who converted him to Christianity. The epistle to Philemon was written on behalf of the slave.

OX. It was used for plowing (1 Kgs 19.19), for drawing wagons (Num 7.3; 2 Sa 6.6), for tramping out grain (Deut 25.4). It was also used for food (1 Kgs 1.25) and for sacrificial purposes (Num 7.87,88; 2 Sam 24.22; 2 Chr 5.6).

P

PALACE. A large house which is the official residence of a sovereign. David built a royal palace in Jerusalem (2 Sam 5.9, 7.1,2). Solomon also constructed a residence of great magnificence which took thirteen years to build.

PALM. A tall, straight tree (Song 7.7,8; Je 10.5). Parts of it were used in various portions of the Temple (1 Kgs 6.29,32,25). The palm leaf was emblematic of peace, also of victory (Jn 12.13; Rev 7.9).

PARABLE. A story or fable for the illustration of moral or religious truth. In order to make the truths of the kingdom more intelligible and impress them upon the memory, Jesus clothed them in images and narrative form.

PARADISE. A word used to denote Heaven. It is the place of the just and the righteous (Lk 23.43; 2 Cor 12.4; Rev 2.7).

PARENTS. While the fifth commandment sets forth the duty of children to parents, the obligations parents sustain to their children are clearly taught. The child should be trained to fear the Lord, and the parent to refrain from provoking their children unnecessarily (Deut 6.7; Eph 6.4).

PASSOVER. The first of the three annual Hebrew festivals at which all the men must appear at the sanctuary (Ex 12.43, 13.3-10; Deut 16.1) and one of two feasts in memory of past events, the other being the feast of tabernacles. It was required that the paschal lamb be without blemish, and was thus typical of Christ (Ex 12.5; 1 Pet 1.18,19). That a bone should not be broken (Ex 12.46, Jn 19.36). It was eaten with unleavened bread (Ex 12.18; 1 Cor 5.8).

PATRIARCH. The founder of a family or a race. In the New Testament it is applied to Abraham, the head of the Messianic nation (Heb 7.4), also to the sons of Jacob (Acts 7.8,9), Jacob, the father of Israel, and to David (Acts 2.29). It applies to the heads of families of the age prior to the time of Moses.

PAUL. The great apostle to the Gentiles. His Hebrew name was Saul which he retained until the time of his visit to Paphos where Sergius Paulus was converted. He was of the tribe of Benjamin, a native of Tarsus. (Acts 9.11, 21.39; 22.3; Phil 3.5). In this intellectual center, the seat of a famous school of philosophy, he was reared under Grecian influences. Like other Jewish boys he was taught a trade, that of tent making (Acts 18.3). In Jerusalem he was trained in the Scriptures by one of the most learned and distinguished rabbis of the day, Gamaliel, grandson of the famous Hillel. Paul was converted during a journey to Damascus where he was planning to persecute the Christians. But the voice of Jesus came to him and this led to his conversion (Acts 9.1-25). Later he participated in three great missionary journeys extending from Jerusalem and Antioch westward through Cyprus and Asia Minor, and even into Europe. Among his traveling companions at various times were Barnabas, John Mark, Silas, and Luke. One of his journeys took him to Rome, where he was held a prisoner. He is believed to have suffered martyrdom in Rome late in the reign of Nero (about A.D. 67). Thirteen letters written by Paul during his lifetime, under the inspiration of the Spirit, are preserved in the New Testament.

PENTATEUCH. The first five books of the Old Testament, called by the Israelites the law (Josh 1.7; Mt 5.17), the law of Moses (Ezra 7.6; Lu 2.22), the book of the law and the book of Moses (John 1.8; 2 Chr 25.3,4).

PENTECOST. See Weeks, Feast of.

PETER. His name was formerly Simon, the son of Jonas (Jn 1.42, 21.15,16). He was a native of Bethsaida (Jo 1.44) but later dwelt at Capernaum (Mt 8.14; Lk 4.38). His brother, Andrew, a disciple of John the Baptist, brought him to Jesus, whose disciple he became (Jn 1.40). He became associated with Jesus (Mt 4.19; Mk 1.17; Lk 5.10) and then became an apostle (Mt 10.2; Lk 6.13,14). He was a man of great earnestness, was self-assertive and impulsive, and had the qualities of leadership. In the lists of the apostles his name is always first (Mt 17.1; Mk 5.37, 9.2, 13.3; Lk 8.51, 9.28). In the fishing industry he was in partnership with Zebedee and his two sons on the Sea of Galilee (Mt 4.18; Mk 1.16; Lk 5.3) but, with James and John, he responded without hesitation to the call of Christ. He, with James and John, beheld the marvelous transfiguration of Christ (Mt 17.1,2) and they were again his companions in the scene of Jesus' agony in Gethsemane (Mt 26.36,37).

PHARISEES. There were three Jewish sects—Pharisees, Sadducess, Essenes (Acts 26.5). This sect arose prior to the period of the Maccabees when there was a tendency on the part of the Jews to adopt Grecian customs. In opposition to this the Pharisees conformed in the strictest manner to the Mosiac institutions. They were distinguished from the Sadducees in their doctrinal beliefs in holding to the doctrine of the resurrection and immortality of the soul, the doctrine of future reward and punishment (Acts 23.8). But conformity to the law was the essential characteristic of their religion. In addition to the Mosaic law they adhered strongly to traditions of the elders. This was denounced by Christ because it nullified the Scriptures (Mt 15.2,3,6). They were denounced by John the Baptist as well as by Christ for their observance of letter of the law instead of the spirit of it (Jn 8.1-11).

PHILIP. 1. One of the Twelve Apostles. He met Jesus beyond the Jordan and was called to be his disciple. Later, he brought Nathanael to Jesus (Jn 1.43-48). It was to him certain Greeks expressed their desire to see Jesus (Jn 12.20,21). 2. Philip the Evangelist. He was one of the seven deacons of the early church (Acts 6.5). When the disciples were dispersed by persecution, he preached in Samaria (Acts 8.4-8, 21.8). He was then divinely directed to go to Gaza where he met, taught, and baptized the eunuch (Acts 8.26-39) and went on to Caesarea (Acts 8.40). His four daughters had the gift of prophecy (Acts 21.8,9). 3. Son of Herod the Great and half-brother of Herod Antipas (Mt 14.3; Lk 3.1).

PHILISTINES. These formidable opponents of Israel, particularly from the time of the judges to David, are not mentioned by name in the New Testament. Against them Samson waged a single-handed contest (Judg 14-16). When the elders of Israel, fearful of defeat, sent the ark to the camp, the Philistines captured but returned it at the outbreak of a plague (1 Sam 4-6). Saul fought them valiantly but was defeated at Mount Gilboa where he and three sons died in battle (1 Sam 31). David defeated and reduced them to vassalage (2 Sam 5.22,25, 8.1).

PILATE, PONTIUS. He was appointed by the Emperor

Tiberius to be procurator of Judea in 26 A.D. (Lk 3.1). Pilate was obstinate and merciless, a hard, cruel man. When duty conflicted with personal interests, the claims of duty were disregarded, as in the case of Jesus. His liberation would have increased Pilate's unpopularity (Mt 27; Lk 23).

POOL. A small body of water fed by springs or rain. Gihon, Bethesda, Siloam were noted pools in Jerusalem (2 Chr 33.14; Jn 5.2, 9.7). There were also pools at Samaria, Heshbon, Hebron, Gibeon (2 Sam 2.13, 4.12; 1 Kgs 22.38; Song 7.4).

POOR. The impoverished, for whom the Mosaic law made ample provision. The poor laws were very explicit. Cancellation of considerable indebtedness was required in years of Jubilee (Lev 25, 27.14-25). A hungry person was permitted to satisfy his immediate needs in the field or vineyard of another (Deut 23.24,25). The poor by law gleaned after the reapers, cut and gathered what was left standing in the fields. Also, the fruit left on the branches was the property of the poor (Lev 19.9,10, 23.22; Deut 24.19-21). The poor should be remembered on joyous occasions and at the time of sacrificial feasts (Deut 16.11,14). Injustice toward the poor was denounced by the prophets (Isa 1.23, 10.2; Ezek 22.7,29; Mal 3.5).

POTTER. One who makes earthenware. After the clay was worked over and made soft and pliable, it was placed on a wheel. As the wheel revolved, the potter shaped the clay with his hand (Isa 41.25). It was then baked in a furnace (Jer 18.3,4). This molding of the clay is used to illustrate the power of God in human affairs (Isa 45.9; Jer 18.5-12; Rom 9.20-25).

PRAYER. The most direct expression of the religious nature in its communion with God. The Bible cites many examples (Gen 4.26; 20.17, 25.21; Ex 32.11). Prayer expresses the innate conviction of the soul of the personality of God. It is a remarkable fact that the great prayers of the

Bible are in the Old Testament—the intercessory prayers of Abraham and Moses (Gen 18.23-32; Ex 32.11-14; Num 14.13-19); the great penitential prayer of David (Ps 51); the prayer of Solomon for wisdom (1 Kgs 3.5-9); Solomon's prayer of dedication of the Temple, one of the greatest prayers of the Bible (1 Kgs 8.23-53); the prayer of Daniel (Dan 9.3-19). Jesus was often in prayer but there is record of only one extended prayer (Jn 17).

PRIEST. At Sinai the office was instituted in the most solemn manner. The tribe of Levi was set apart for religious service. The priesthood was made hereditary in the family of Aaron (Ex 28.1, 40.12-15; Deut 10.6; 1 Kgs 8.4; Ezra 2.36). When Aaron died, his oldest living son, Eleazar, succeeded him in the high priesthood (Num 20.25-28; Deut 10.6) and he was succeeded by his son Phinehas (Judg 20.28; 1 Chr 6.4-50).

PRISON. A place for the confinement of criminals. Prisons had no place in the penal system of the ancient Hebrews. Joseph's imprisonment was in Egypt and Samson's was in Philistia (Gen 39.20,23, 40.3,5; Judg 16.21,25). From the time of Jeremiah, mention is made of dungeons and pits in the sense of prisons (Jer 37.16, 38.6; Zech 9.11). In New Testament times the prisons were patterned after Greek and Roman models. There were prison rooms in the palace of Herod and the palace at Caesarea (Acts 12.6,10, 26.10).

PROCONSUL. The governor of a Roman province (Acts 13.7, 18.12, 19.38).

PROCURATOR. The administrator of a province under the Roman emperor; also called chief magistrate and governor (Acts 24.27).

PROPHET. A divinely inspired minister of Jehovah; originally called a seer (1 Sam 9.9). Abraham, Aaron, and others were considered prophets but it was not until Samuel that prophecy came into its own. In the period from Samuel to Elisha the so-called schools of the prophets were established in important commercial centers. Until the period of the Exile the prophets were advisers to kings. In this capacity they never hesitated to administer a deserved rebuke to the monarch. In their writings the prophets consistently attacked unrighteousness, self-indulgence, and greed. They stood for monothesism and sometimes they predicted future events. Prophecy reached its peak with the Messianic prophecy. Prophets and prophecy are mentioned in the New Testament. Jesus was a prophet (Mt 13.57, 21.11; Lk 13.33).

PROPHETESS. A woman divinely called to prophesy. Such was Miriam (Ex 15.20, 21; Num 12.2; Mic 6.4), Deborah (Judg 4.4,5,6,14), Huldah (2 Kgs 22.14-20), and the daughters of Philip, the evangelist .9).

PROSELYTE. A New Testament term designating a convert to Judaism (Acts 6.5, 8.27).

PROVINCE. An administrative district either within or without the confines of the controlling nation. The provinces of the Bible were usually subject to Baylonia, Persia, or Rome.

PUBLICAN. A member of a company to which the Romans auctioned off the right to collect taxes. Publicans were engaged to do the actual collecting of the customs. The system afforded opportunity for extortion, while doubtless there were some exceptions (Lk 3.12,13, 19.8). A Jewish publican was a social outcast, looked upon with contempt, for raising taxes for a foreign and heathen government. Zacchaeus, a Jew, had charge of the revenues of Jericho (Lk 19.1,2).

PURIFICATION. The process by which a person ceremonially unclean was made clean again. Contact with a dead body, for example, rendered one unclean under the Mosaic law and purification by the ashes of a heifer was necessary (Num 19). Purification for certain bodily disorders was required in the form of cleansing and offering of a burnt offering (Lev 15; Num 5.2,3). Following childbirth, the mother was placed under rigid requirements not to touch a hallowed thing or to enter the sanctuary (Lev 12.8; Lk 2.21.24).

R

RABBI, RABBONI. A title of respect given by the Jews to their teachers (Mt 23.7; Jn 1.38). It was also applied to doctors and other learned persons. It was often used for Jesus (Jn 1.38,49, 3.2, 6.25, 20.16) and once for John the Baptist (Jn 3.26).

RACHEL. Laban's younger daughter whom Jacob loved when he first met her in Mesopotamia. To secure her as his wife he served Laban seven years. He was tricked by Laban who insisted that he should marry Leah, the older daughter. This he did, and served another seven years to marry Rachel (Gen 29.1-30). She had two sons, Joseph and Benjamin, but died giving birth to the latter in Canaan. Benjamin was the only one of the twelve sons born in the Land of Promise. Her burial place is near Bethlehem (Gen 30.22-25, 35.16-18).

RAHAB. A woman who lived in Jericho, whose house was on the wall. When Joshua sent spies to the city she concealed them and enabled them to escape by lowering them by a cord on the outside of the wall (Josh 2,1-24). She and her family were spared when the city fell and became part of the chosen people (Josh 6.22-25; Heb 11.31; Jas 2.25).

RAINBOW. A beautiful arc exhibiting the colors of the spectrum, formed opposite the sun by the refraction and reflection of the sun's rays on rain drops or mist. In Genesis, God tells Noah that the rainbow is the symbol of the convenant between God, Noah, and every living creature (Gen 9.12-17; Rev 4.3).

RAM. A male sheep. One of the clean animals the Jews were permitted to eat (Gen 31.38). They were used as burnt or peace offerings (Gen 22.13; Lev 1:10, 8.18) and also as a sin offering (Lev 5.15, 6.6). The skin of the ram was used for covering the tabernacle (Ex 26.14).

REBEKAH. The servant of Abraham was sent to Mesopotamia to secure a wife for Isaac. He met Rebekah at a well and was impressed by her beauty. In her home he explained his mission and she agreed to return with him to Canaan. She became the wife of Isaac and the mother of Esau and Jacob (Gen 24.1-67). Jacob was her favorite. With him she contrived to deceive Isaac and secured for Jacob the blessing (Gen 25.28, 27.1-28.5).

RECONCILIATION. To establish a state of peace between two persons, or between God and man by the atoning work of Christ. The latter is the Biblical sense of the term. It embraces two ideas, the first of which is that of God being reconciled to man. It denotes that necessary attitude of opposition to sin on the part of God, and that in order to pardon and receive the sinner, the demands of justice and holiness must be met. God made this possible by sending his Son that sinners might be reconciled to God (Jn 3.16; Rom 5.6-21). The second fact is that of man being reconciled to God. This is accomplished when man accepts the provision God has made for his salvation; at that moment there is a cessation of his enmity to God (2 Cor 5.18-21).

REDEMPTION. It denotes release, freedom, by the payment of a price. Redemption implies bondage, that from which we are redeemed; bondage to the curse and dominion of sin (Gal 3.13); bondage of death as the penalty of sin (Acts 26.18; Heb 2.14,15). To effect this redemption Christ is man's Redeemer. He paid the redemption price, his atoning work, the price paid for human redemption. By this we are made free, redeemed from the curse of the law upon sin. When we accept him, Satan's power and dominion are broken. We have the power to lead a new, a holy, a free life, and death has lost its sting and terror. This redemption embraces not only that of the soul, but the redemption of the body (Rom 8.15-23; 1 Cor 15.55-57; Eph 1.7; 2 Tim 2.26; Heb 2.9).

RED SEA. To the Hebrews it was known as the "Sea of Weeds." It was crossed by the Israelites when they escaped from the Egyptians (Ex 14.16; Num 33.8; Deut 11.4; Acts 7.36).

REGENERATION. Being born anew (Jn 3.3; 1 Pet 1.23), born of God (1 Jn. 5.1,4), and born of the Spirit (Jn 3.6) are some of the terms used in the Scriptures to express the idea of regeneration. Regeneration is not to be confused with sanctification. The new nature originated and effected by the Holy Spirit (regeneration) is now by the operations of the Spirit developed in its growth in grace in which the spiritual life is brought to perfection (sanctification). The one is the beginning of the new life, the other the development and consummation of it. The regenerated man becomes a new creature (2 Cor 5.17) with new power (Acts 1.8) and with spiritual attitudes (Gal 5.18-25; Eph 4.22-32; Col 3.8-24; 1 Pet 3.8-18; 2 Pet 1.5-8; 1 Jn 3.9-17, 4.7,20,21, 5.1-8).

REHOBOAM. When Rehoboam assumed the throne, the representatives of the tribes asked him to lessen their tax burdens. The king countered with a plan to tax them even more. As a result ten tribes withdrew from the nation. Rehoboam reigned for seventeen years during which time his country was invaded by Shishak of Egypt who seized Jerusalem and other cities. Rehoboam and his nation reverted to idolatry (1 Kgs 11.43-15.6; 2 Chr 9.31-13.7).

REMNANT. The portion of Israel which was preserved to form a renewed Israel—one which would replace the nation upon which judgment had fallen (Isa 4.2-6; 10.20-23; 12.6; Jer 23.3, 32.36-44; Am 9.8-15; Mic 4.6-8; 8.12).

RESURRECTION. The doctrine of the reunion of body and soul having been separated by death. In the time of Christ it was a doctrine of the Jews, but denied by the Sadducees (Mt 22.30; Lk 20.39; Jn 11.24; Acts 23.6,8). It was specifically taught by the apostles (1 Cor 15; Phil

3.20,21; 1 Thess 4.14; Rev 20.6-14). The Scriptures clearly teach the body shall rise again having its identity preserved; that it will be a glorious body, like the glorified body of Christ, and will endure with the soul through all eternity. The resurrection of Christ is the first fruits of the resurrection and the guarantee of our resurrection in the likeness of his body.

REUBEN. 1. The eldest son of Jacob by Leah, Jacob's first wife (Gen 29.31,32, 35.23, 46.8). It was Reuben who saved the life of his brother, Joseph, when the other brothers wished to kill him. Reuben suggested putting him in a pit for it was his plan to return Joseph to his father when the other brothers left the scene. However, before Reuben was able to rescue him, Joseph was sold to the Midianites (Gen 37.21-29). 2. The tribe of Reuben. The request of the Reubenites and Gadites that they have assigned them the district east of the Jordan was granted on condition that they would do their part in the taking of the land. This they did (Num 32.1-42; Josh 4.12, 18.7).

ROME. The capital and chief city of Italy. Eventually the city dominated much of Europe, Asia, and north Africa. It was first a kingdom, then a republic, then an empire. Tiberius was on the throne during the time of Christ's ministry and at the time of his death (Lk 2.1, 3.1,2). Under Nero the persecution of the Christians was instituted. This continued until the reign of Constantine, who made Christianity the state religion in A.D. 313.

S

SABBATH. The day on which labor ceases. It occurs on the seventh day of the week because according to Genesis that was the day on which the Lord rested after creating the world (Gen 2.1-3). It was at Sinai that the law was first announced relative to maintaining the sanctity of the Sabbath. It was the fourth commandment (Ex 20.8-11, 31.16-18; Deut 5.15). It was to be a holy convocation for divine worship (Lev 23.3), a sign indicating they were sanctified by Jehovah (Ex 31.13). In the time of Christ the Pharisees applied the law regarding Sabbath observance in the most scrupulous manner with the result that they missed the whole spirit and purpose of the Sabbath. In opposition to them in the performance of works of necessity and mercy, our Lord stated that the Sabbath was made for man, that the Son of man is not the slave but the lord of the Sabbath. (Mk 2.27; Lk 13.14, 14.3,5; Jn 5.10).

SACKCLOTH. A coarse dark cloth made of goat's hair (Isa 50.3; Rev 6.12), the garment of mourners (2 Sam 3.31; 2 Kgs 19.1,2), often of prophets (Isa 20.2). It had the appearance of a sack and was usually worn over the other garments (Jon 3.6).

SADDUCEES. One of the Jewish religious parties in existence at the time of Christ. This sect did not believe in the resurrection and a future state of the soul, nor did it believe in the theory of rewards or punishment after death. In these beliefs it was opposed by the Pharisees, another important Jewish religious party. Politically the Sadducees favored the policies of Rome in the government of Palestine. This was the party of the priesthood, for about 200 years prior to the fall of Jerusalem (A.D. 70). Most of the high priests were drawn from its ranks. John the Baptist once called both the Sadducees and the Pharisees a brood of vipers (Mt. 3.7), and Jesus warned his disciples against their doctrines (Mt 16.1-12).

SALOME. Daughter of Herodias and Philip. Her mother left Philip for his half-brother, Herod Antipas, the man who imprisoned John the Baptist. Salome so delighted Antipas with her dancing that he offered to gratify any wish. Her mother instructed her to ask for the head of John the Baptist. Her request was granted (Mt 14.6).

SALVATION. The general idea of deliverance, safety, a state of security being effected, saved. In the Old Testament God's people are delivered by him from foes and from the devices of the wicked (Ps 37.40, 59.2, 106.4). It is also expressed in sins being forgiven, in prayers being answered (Ps 51.12, 69.13, 79.9). The thought of the New Testament doctrine of salvation's deliverance from the state and consequences of sin by the saving work of Christ alone (Mt 1.21; Acts 4.12; Heb 2.10, 5.9), made efficacious to us by faith and acceptance (Jn 3.16; Heb 2.3). The motive in providing such salvation is the love of God, but it is made possible by the holiness of Christ who offered himself without spot or blemish for our salvation.

SAMARIA. The capital of the northern kingdom of Israel. Samaria was the scene of many of the events in the history of the northern kingdom. The city was besieged several times and was almost starved into submission by Ben-hadead (1 Kgs 20.1; 2 Kgs 6.8-7.20). During the reign of Ahab and his wife Jezebel, a temple was built to Baal and idolatry flourished. Because of the idolatry, the prophets threatened Samaria with destruction (Is 7.9, 28.1-4; Hos 8.5-14; Am 3.9-15). In 722 B.C. the city was captured by the Assyrians after a three-year siege.

SAMARITANS. The Samaritans were a mixed race, composed of imported colonists and the Israelites who remained when the bulk of the Ten Tribes were carried into captivity. They had a temple to Jehovah, they accepted Moses as their lawgiver and the Pentateuch as their law, but they rejected the traditions and rules of the Pharisees. They observed the rite of circumcision, the requirements of the Sabbath, and the yearly Jewish festivals, but denied the Jewish priesthood, and refused to accept Jerusalem as the one place where the temple of Jehovah should stand. After the return from captivity there was considerable bitterness between the Jews and the Samaritans. To pious Jews the term "Samaritan" was a term of reproach. (Lk 10.30-37, 17.11-19; Jn 4.9, 39-40, 8.48).

SAMSON. An outstanding judge of Israel. He was destined to deliver his people from the oppression of the Philistines which was felt especially by Judah and Dan. Samson possessed marvelous physical strength which he used against the Philistines but was not correspondingly morally strong. After Samson set the foxes loose in the fields of the Philistines, the Philistines demanded that Samson be surrendered to them (Judg 14.1-15.5). He allowed himself to be bound by his cowardly countrymen who failed to realize that he was their deliverer, but breaking the bands, he slew a thousand of his foes. Samson courted a Philistine woman, Delilah, and at length told her the source of his strength was his hair. While he was asleep, she cut his hair. Unable any longer to resist his Philistine enemies, he was taken prisoner and blinded (Judg 16.16-30).

SAMUEL. The son of Elkanah and Hannah (1 Sam 1.1; 1 Chr 6.26,35). Following the death of Eli, Samuel, the prophet, became the chief religious authority in the land. In his administration the moral and religious state of things greatly improved.

SANCTIFICATION. It signifies setting apart for a sacred purpose. In the Mosaic system there were sacred persons, as the high priest, sacred things, as the tabernacle, sacred seasons, as the passover and day of atonement. Sanctification is to be distinguished from justification and regeneration. Justification signifies the judicial relation of the sinner to God, and regeneration the changed nature of the sinner by the agency of the Holy Spirit. Sanctification denotes the carrying forward of that work of grace in the soul to its completeness (Rom 6.11; Phil 1.6; 1 Pet 2.24).

SARAH. The wife of Abraham; also his half sister (Gen 20.12). She was ten years younger than he. She came with him from Ur of the Chaldees (Gen 11.28-31, 17.17). In Egypt Abraham, afraid men would slay him in order to marry her, introduced her as his sister (Gen 12.10-20) and repeated it years later in Gerar (Gen 20.1-18). In both instances it brought trouble. Abraham was divinely promised an heir. Sarah, at the age of 75, thinking she was in the way of the fulfillment of the convenant promise, urged Abraham to make Hagar, Sarah's Egyptian maid, a secondary wife, which he did and Ishmael was born (Gen 16.1-16). When she was 89, God promised her a son (Gen 17.1-19; Heb 11.11,12) and Isaac was born—the child of promise. At this time her name was changed from Sarai to Sarah (Gen 17.15-22, 18.9-15, 21.1-5).

SATAN. Satan is mentioned first by name in Job 1.6-12, 2.1. He is mentioned as a personality in Zech 3.1 and Christ called him by this name in the third temptation (Mt 4.10). He is called the devil (Mt 4.1; Mk 1.13), and as adversary, he is characterized as hostile to God and man (Job 2.3; Lk 22.3) in his attempt to destroy the work of God (Mk 4.15) and to induce men to sin (Acts 5.3, 26.18). His first appearance in the history of mankind was in Eden as the seducer of Adam and Eve (Gen 3.1-6; 2 Cor 11.3; Rev 12.9). Christ declared he was a murderer from the beginning (Jn 8.44). He inspired Judas to betray his Lord (Jn 13.27; Lk 22.3). It is in the New Testament, especially, that the personality, character, and activities of Satan are set forth. He is the ruler of a kingdom, invested with powers and rules demons (Mt. 12.24,26; Lk 11.18; Rev 12.7). He is the god of this world seeking to enslave men to serve him (Lk 22.3; Acts 26.18; 2 Cor 4.4; 2 Thess 2.9; Rev 12.9).

SAUL. 1. The first king of Israel. He was a faithful worshipper of Jehovah as well a a man of considerable military ability. It was following his victory over the Ammonites at Jabesh-gilead that he was made king (1 Sam 11.1-15). Saul took his own life after the Hebrews were defeated by the Philistines (1 Sam 31.1-10). 2. The name of the apostle Paul before his conversion (Acts 7.58).

SAVIOR. One who saves, a deliverer from danger or evil. In the Old Testament God is the savior, deliverer of the covenant people (Ps 106.21; Isa 43.3,11, 45.15,21, 63.8; Jer 14.8; Hos 13.4). The word applies especially to Jesus Christ who was called Savior by the angel announcing his birth (Lk 2.11), by some Samaritans (Jn 4.42), by Paul (Phil 3.20), and by others (Acts 5.31; 2 Pet 2.20; 1 Jn 4.14).

SCEPTRE. A staff or rod which served as an emblem of authority, especially for royalty (Ps 45.6; Am 1.5; Heb 1.8). Among such ancients as the Egyptians and Persians it was a rod, probably about five feet long bearing at one end an ornamental ball or other figure.

SCOURGE. To punish or torture, particularly by lashing. Mosaic law permitted but forty lashes as punishment (Deut 25.2,3). Paul said that he received from the Jews 39 stripes five different times (2 Cor 11.24). Under Roman law Roman citizens could be beaten but not scourged and once Paul saved himself from scourging by the Romans by revealing his Roman citizenship (Acts 22.24-30).

SCRIBE. A public writer. As one who copied the Scriptures, Ezra was the most distinctive of Old Testament scribes (Ezra 7.6.10). He also taught the statutes of the law. In New Testament times scribes were the interpreters and teachers of the law. They held the highest place among the people, many members of the Sanhedrin being of this class (Mt 16.21, 26.3). They had the respect and reverence of the people. They bitterly opposed Jesus (Mt 21.15) and he denounced them (Lk 11.44).

SEAL. A design or name of the owner inscribed into a signet ring. It was made of preicous stone, metal, or clay and could also be worn about the neck. The seal, which leaves an impression in wax or clay, was used to fasten documents and letters. If the seal was unbroken it was certain the letter or document had not been opened.

SENNACHERIB. Son of Sargon. He ascended the throne of Assyria when his father was assassinated (705 B.C.) About twenty years after the capture of Samaria by his father, he invaded Judah and according to his account he captured 46 towns and carried away over 200,000 captives. Later he again captured Babylon and massacred the people (2 Kgs 18.13, 19.16, 20, 36; 2 Chr 32; Isa 37).

SEPTUAGINT. A Greek translation of the Old Testament made at Alexandria for Greek-speaking Jews. The oldest of versions of the Bible, the Septuagint was finished about the beginning of the Christian era and became the Bible of the early Christian church. It was made by seventy translators, hence its name and designation - LXX.

SERMON ON THE MOUNT. The customary designation for the teachings of Jesus recorded in Mt 5-7. The mountain on which Jesus gave the sermon to his disciples has been identified with twin peaks west of Tiberias.

SERVANT OF JEHOVAH. One who acknowledges God and performs his will. Thus Moses was the servant of God (Ps 105.26), and David (Ps 132.10) and Abraham (Ps 105.6). The servant of Jehovah is depicted in Isa 52.13-53.12 as having suffered affliction and death, thereby atoning for the sins of man. Most commentators hold that the servant here is Christ, the Messiah.

SETH. Third son of Adam. He was born after the murder of Abel by Cain. Seth was the head of the genealogical line which produced Jesus (Lk 3.38). He died at the age of 912 (Gen 5.6-8).

SHEEP. An animal extensively raised in Palestine for its wool, skin, meat, and milk. It was a ceremonially clean animal much used in sacrifice (Lev 1.10, 4.32, 5.15, 22.21). The Hebrews in the patriarchial age were shepherds (Gen 12.16) as were their descendants who settled in Canaan after the Exodus (1 Chr 27.31). Angels appeared to certain shepherds at the time of the birth of Christ (Lk 2.8-16). Trumpets were made of the horns of rams (Josh 6.4).

SHEPHERD. A herder of sheep. In Biblical times he led them to pasture, to watering places, and at night to the fold. He was responsible for driving away attacking wild beasts (1 Sam 17.34-36). The patriarchs of Genesis were shepherds (Gen 13.6). Jesus called himself the good shepherd (Jn 10.14).

SHOE. Sandals strapped to the feet by latchets. They were not worn at meals or in the living room (Lk 7.38). When the guest entered, the shoes were removed by a servant (Mk 1.7). When on what was regarded as holy ground, sandals were removed (Ex 3.5; Josh 5.15). The same was true of the priests in the performance of their duties in the sanctuary.

SILAS. A member of the church at Jerusalem (Acts 15.22), probably a Hellenistic Jew. He was commissioned by the Council at Jerusalem to report its decision about circumcision to the church of Antioch (Acts 15.22,27,32). When Paul and Barnabas disagreed regarding Mark, Silas became Paul's companion on the second journey (Acts 15.40). At Philippi they were imprisoned (Acts 16.19,25). He remained with Timothy at Berea and both joined Paul at Corinth (Acts 18.5).

SIMEON. 1. The second son of Jacob. His mother was Leah (Gen 29.33). After Shechem defiled Simeon's sister, Dinah, Levi and Simeon massacred the inhabitants of the city of Shechem. Later Jacob deplored this deed (Gen 34.24-31, 49.5-7). 2. A tribe descended by the sons of Simeon. The tribe was located in the extreme south of Judah and eventually was absorbed by the tribe of Judah (Josh 19.1,2,9). 3. A devout man who had been divinely assured that he would not die until he had seen Jesus. When Jesus was but a boy, Simeon saw him (Lk 2.25-35).

SIMON. 1. Simon Peter. See PETER. 2. Simon the Zealot, called "Simon the Canaanite," one of the apostles (Lk 6.15; Acts 1.13). 3. A Pharisee in whose house Christ was a guest at the time a sinful woman anointed his feet (Lk 7.36-50). 4. Simon the Cyrene, father of Alexander and Rufus (Mk 15.21). When Jesus fell under the weight of his cross on the way to Calvary, it was placed upon Simon (Mt 27.32). 5. Simon the sorcerer, usually called Simon Magnus. A magician of Samaria, he was converted to Christianity by the preaching of Philip. He was severely rebuked by Peter when he offered to purchase the wonder-working power of the Holy Spirit (Acts 8.9-24). 6. Simon the tanner. He lived at Joppa. He was a Christian (Acts 9.43, 10.6, 17,32).

SIN. "Missing the mark." It is defined as "Any want of conformity unto, or transgression of the law of God." Sin is transgression of the divine law; where no law is, there is no transgression (Rom 4.15). There are two forms of sin—*a sin of commission*, the doing of anything forbidden by the law; *a sin of omission*, not doing what the law requires. The effect of Adam's sin upon the moral life of the Adamic race is what is meant by original sin, the consequences of that sin being universal (Rom 5.12). The Bible clearly states that all have sinned (Rom 3.9,10,23, 5.12; Gal 3.22; 1 Jn 1.8). The wages of sin is death (Gen 2.15-17; Ezek 18.20; Rom 6.23; 8.2; Jas 1.13-15) unless man accepts the atonement provided by God through his son, Jesus Christ (Isa 53.5; Jn 3.14-18; Rom 3.25; 1 Jn 1.5-2.2). Jesus said that sin originated in the heart (Mt 15.11; Mk 7.15) and warned against sin against the Holy Spirit (Mt 12.30-32; Lk 12.8-10; Jn 16.7-11). This sin is unpardonable, not because God cannot or will not forgive it, but because the sinner refuses to be led by the Spirit to accept the terms of forgiveness (Isa 59.1-3; Eph 4.30; 1 Thess 5.19; Heb 3.7-19; 10.26,27; 1 Pet 2).

SLAVE. Slavery an ancient institution. One might be purchased (Gen 37.28,36; Ezek 27.13). One might become a slave because of inability to pay a debt, but to enslave a debtor or his children was against the Mosaic law (Ex 22.3; 2 Kgs 4.1; Am 2.6). One might sell himself, or a child (Ex 21.2,7; Lev 25.39,47). The brothers of Joseph sold him for twenty pieces of silver (Gen 37.28). The Jewish laws safeguarded the treatment of Hebrew slaves, and after six years of service he might have his freedom. In the year of Jubilee all Hebrew slaves were liberated (Lev 25.40). Under Christian conditions obedience was enjoined (Eph 6.5-8; Col 3.22-25). The master was also enjoined to recognize the rights of the slave (Eph 6.9; Col 4.1).

SODOM. One of the five cities of the plain of the Jordan (Gen 13.10). It was famous for its wickedness (Gen 13.13, 18.20; Isa 3.9; La 4.6). It was the home of Lot and his family. However, before the Lord destroyed the city because of its evilness, Lot was allowed to escape with all of his family except his wife who turned to salt as she gazed back at the city (Gen 19.1-26).

SOLOMON. The son of David and Bathsheba; born in Jerusalem. He was king of united Israel (973?-933? B.C.). As king he strengthened the fortifications of Jerusalem, and embellished it with royal buildings and the famous Temple (1 Kgs 9.15,24, 11.27). He had a large army with many chariots and horsemen (1 Kgs 4.26, 10.26) and he also controlled a navy and a lucrative sea trade. His reign was one of luxury and extravagance. He began his career as a king renowned for his wisdom (1 Kgs 3.3-14). He was author of 3000 proverbs and 1005 songs (1 Kgs 4.32). However, later he lapsed into idolatry, an occurrence attributed to the influence of his wives (1 Kgs 11.4). He died after a forty-year rule and was succeeded by his son, Rehoboam (1 Kgs 11.42,43).

SON OF GOD. The sonship of Christ. In the N.T. it occurs nearly fifty times and is expressive of the relation that exists between the Father and the eternal Son (Mt 16.16, 27.43; Mk 1.1; Jn 3.18) He has all the perfections of God, and equal with God (Jn 1.1-14, 5.17-25; Phil 2.6). In receiving the commission of the Father, in his mode of operation he is subordinate, but not inferior (Jn 3.1,17, 8.42; Gen 4.4; Heb 1.2). It was because he claimed he was the son of God, that he was charged with blasphemy by the Sanhedrin (Mt 26.63-66; Mk 14.61). At his baptism and transfiguration he was divinely acknowledged as the Son of God (Mt 3.16,17, 17.5).

SON OF MAN. This title was applied by Christ to himself. In his use of it it does not denote that he was merely human and not divine for he frequently declared the latter. He identified himself with man in his human nature and in his sufferings for mankind (Mt 20.28, Jn. 1.14).

SORCERER. One who practices sorcery. His power is allegedly gained from the aid or control of evil spirits, particularly for purposes of gaining hidden knowledge (Ex

7.11; Dan 2.2; Rev 21.8, 22.15). He does not foretell the future but rather compels it or determines fate by means of his incantations, potions, or magical charms. Sorcerers were common in Egypt, Assyria, and Babylon (Isa 47.9,12; Dan 2.2) but they were banned from Israel (Deut 18.10-12). They were also called witches and were punishable by death (Ex 22.18). Simon Magnus and Bar-jesus were prominent sorcerers in New Testament times (Acts 8.9-24, 13.6-12).

SOWER. One who scatters seeds. While sowing the sower walked down a furrow distributing the seed with his hand. Jesus referred to a sower in one of his parables (Mt 13.4). The seed was supposed to be ceremonially clean and mixed seed was not to be sown in the same field (Lev 11.37,38, 19.19; Deut 22.9).

STAR. It is not strange that the stars, on account of their number, and constellations, should have attracted the attention of the ancients (Gen 22.17; Isa 13.10). With the exception of the sun and moon all heavenly bodies were designated stars by the Hebrews. They recognized the stars as the handiwork of God (Ps 8.3) and under his power (Isa 13.10; Jer 31.35). But apart from the ordinary observations of the heavens there is nothing in the Scriptures to show that the ancient Hebrews had any real knowledge of astronomy. Following the heathen nations, Israelites who left the pure worship of Jehovah, made the stars objects of worship (Deut 4.19; 2 Kgs 17.16, 23.5).

STEPHEN. He is first mentioned in connection with his appointment as one of seven deacons of the church of Jerusalem (Acts 6.5). He was a man of great faith (Acts 6.8). The activities of Stephen aroused the opposition of foreign Jews who had synagogues in Jerusalem. They charged Stephen with blasphemy. They claimed to have heard him say that Jesus would set aside the Mosiac institutions (Acts 6.11-14). Those who testified against him were false witnesses (Acts 6.13). In his defense (Acts 7.2-60), he set forth God's selection of Israel for divine ends but he pointed out that the Israelites were often in opposition to God and his purpose. When he said that he saw Christ, they rushed upon him to put him to death. With Saul of Tarsus holding the clothes of the mob, they stoned him to death. Stephen was the first Christian martyr.

STONE. A piece of detached rock. Palestine is a stony country having limestone, sandstone, marble, and flint. Stone was particularly useful in ancient times as a building material. The Phoenicians were well known for their ability to cut stone for building purposes (2 Sam 5.11). Stones were used in memorial pillars (Gen 28.18, 31.45, 35.14; Josh 4.9; 1 Sam 7.12). They were used to close the entrances to tombs (Mt 27.60; Josh 11.38) and caves (Josh 10.18; Dan 6.17). By means of catapults and slings they were hurled as missiles (1 Sam 17.40,49; 2 Chr 26.14,15). Boundary marks and scale weights were normally made of stone (Deut 19.14, 25.13).

STONING. This was the usual mode of inflicting capital punishment provided by the Mosaic law. The witnesses placed their hands on the head of the criminal to indicate he was the bearer of his guilt (Lev 24.14) and the first stones were hurled by the witnesses (Deut 13.9; Jn 8.7). The law required death by stoning for eighteen different crimes including idolatry, wizardry, blasphemy, and Sabbath breaking (Lev 20.27, 24.16; Num 15.32-36; Deut 17.2-5).

SUN. A radiant heavenly body around which the earth and other planets revolve. In the account of its creation it is described as "the greater light to rule the day" (Gen 1.16). It was referred to as the vital power bringing forth vegetation (Deut 33.14; 2 Sam 23.4) and was represented as rising and setting and as moving (2 Kgs 20.11; Ps 19.4-6; Hab 3.11). Joshua's request that the sun stay up until the Israelites defeated the Amorites was granted (Josh 10.12, 13). Many of the peoples with whom the Israelites came in contact worshipped the sun. The Egyptian sun god was called Ra; the Phoenician, Baal; and the Assyrian, Shamash. In Mal 4.2 the promised Messiah was called the "sun of righteousness."

SYNAGOGUE (assembly). A local assembly of Jews organized chiefly for worship; also its building or place of meeting. With the destruction of the Temple by Nebuchadnezzar (586 B.C.) came the necessity for a religious institution which would supplant the one destroyed. The synagoge was accordingly instituted during or soon after the Exile. In its services emphasis shifted from sacrifice to teaching the law and the prophets. Its ultimate origin is veiled in obscurity. The furniture consisted chiefly of a chest (ark) in which were kept the sacred rolls of the law and the prophets. In front of the chest a lamp burned continually. There was usually a raised platform on which stood the reader's desk. There were benches for the worshippers. A few of these, placed in front of the platform and facing the audience, were the "chief seats" in which the Pharisees coveted the honor to sit (Mt 23.6). The service was in four parts as follows: (*a*) recitation of three brief passages of the law including Deut 6.4-9; (*b*) prayer; (*c*) reading from the law and the prophets; and (*d*) pronouncement of the priestly benediction (Num 6.24-26). The reading in Hebrew was accompanied by an interpretation into Aramaic. Eventually, a sermon was included in the service. Visitors, as Paul, were sometimes asked to address the synagoge (Acts 13.14-16).

T

TABERNACLE. A portable sanctuary carried by the Israelites throughout their wilderness wanderings. The Pentateuch describes it as a large tent thirty cubits long, ten cubits broad, with sides ten cubits high. It was the visible symbol of God's presence. When Moses entered this Tabernacle, the cloudy pillar would descend to the doorway and the Lord would talk with Moses face to face (Ex 33.7-11). Elaborate directions for its construction (together with that of its furniture) were divinely given to Moses at Sinai (Ex 25-27,30,31,35-40). The structure was built according to pattern (Ex 25.9,40). Forming the outside portion of the square Israelitish camp were the tents of the twelve tribes. Inside this square were stationed the priests and Levites. The center was the court of the Tabernacle (Ex 27.9) Within the court was the Tabernacle, consisting of a holy place and a Holy of Holies.

TAXES. In the time of the judges the Jews were obliged to pay tithes and the redemption money of the firstborn. The tabernacle and priesthood were thus provided for and also the Levites. Under the monarchy, to meet the great expenditure, heavier taxes were imposed by Solomon on live stock and products of the field (1 Kgs 4.7-28). These measures became oppressive and contributed largely to the division of the kingdom under Rehoboam (1 Kgs 12.4). During the Roman period taxes were collected by a member of a company which purchased the right from the government to collect taxes in a certain region. Called publicans in the Roman period, these men were hated by the people because of their harsh methods.

TEMPLE. 1. *The Solomonic Temple.* The permanent house of the Lord in Jerusalem proposed by David who purchased the site and gathered much of the materials (2 Sam 7; 1 Kgs 5.3-5, 8.17; 1 Chr 22, 28.11-29.9). It was built by Solomon on a Jerusalem hilltop, west of Kidron and north of the ancient city of David, the site likewise occupied by the Temple of Zerubbabel and that of Herod. It was a small oblong building about 45 feet high with inner dimensions of 30x90 feet. The Temple building was divided into two chambers by a partition of olive wood. The chamber on the east corresponded to the Holy Place in the tabernacle. The west chamber, called oracle, corresponded to the Holy of Holies (1 Kgs 6.2,3, 20,31). The walls of both chambers were of cedar and the floor was overlaid with gold (1 Kgs 6.9,15-22, 29-35). Within the oracle were two giant cherubim of olive wood overlaid with gold, and about fifteen feet high. Their outstretched wings were spread above the ark (1 Kgs 6.20,22, 8.5-7). This building was plundered and destroyed by Nebuchadnezzar in 586 B.C. 2. *Zerubbabel's Temple.* The erection of this structure was authorized by Cyrus after Zerubbabel led back to Jerusalem about 50,000 people. It was begun about 520 B.C. (Hag 1.1-4,8) and was finished about four years later. It differed with its predecessor, Solomon's Temple, chiefly in regard to simplicilty. The wooden partition between the holy place and the Holy of Holies was replaced by a veil. One golden candlestick instead of ten stood in the holy place. The ark, which had been destroyed, was not replaced. 3. *Herodian Temple.* To secure the favor of the Jews, Herod the Great promised them a new Temple. Before the second Temple was taken down, the materials for the new temple were gathered. Work on this temple began in 19 B.C. After eighteen months the main building was constructed but the entire work including buildings and courts was not completed until about A.D. 64 or six years before it was destroyed. It was the costliest, the greatest, and most magnificent of the three temples. It was the Temple of New Testament times and to it Jesus was brought as an infant (Lk 2.22-34). Later he taught in it (Mk 14.49). This Temple was the scene of the driving out of the money-changers by Jesus (Mt 21.12-14; Mk 11.15-17; Lk 19.45-47; Jn 2.13-16). This Temple was destroyed in A.D. 70 by the Romans.

TEN COMMANDMENTS. Divinely inscribed on two tablets of stone on Sinai (Ex 20.1-17, 31.18).

TESTAMENT. The Greek word *diatheke* is thus rendered, denoting a covenant, a will (Heb 7.6-10,13, 9.1,4,16,17). The word is used to designate the two portions of the Bible.

TETRARCH. Originally the ruler of the fourth part of a country. The term also applied to subordinate princes or petty kings. The title was applied to Herod Antipas, ruler of Galilee and Perea (Mt 14.1; Lk 3.1,19, 9.7; Acts 13.1).

THEOPHILUS. The person to whom Luke addressed the Acts of the Apostles and the Gospel according to St. Luke (Lk 1.3; Acts 1.1).

THIEF. The designation of anyone who takes what does not belong to him. He may be a petty thief or highwayman (Mt 6.20; Lk 10.30; Jn 12.6). The penalty for stealing under the Mosaic law was that twice the amount of what was stolen must be returned or the thief could be made to serve as a slave until the amount was earned.

THOMAS. An apostle who was also called Didymus, the Greek form of his name (Ma 10.3). It was he who expressed concern for the safety of Jesus when the latter went to Bethany at the time of the death of Lazarus. Thomas proposed that all the apostles go with Jesus and die with him if necessary (Jn 11.16). Known for his doubting nature, Thomas refused to believe the testimony of the others regarding the resurrection of Jesus. He preferred to trust only his own senses (Jn 20.24,25).

THRONE. An elevated seat occupied by a person of authority. He may be a king, a governor, a military officer, a high priest, a judge (1 Sam 1.9; 2 Sam 3.10; Ps 122.5; Jer 1.15; Mt 19.28). Solomon's throne, overlaid with gold and inlaid with ivory, was six steps from the ground and a stone lion stood at each end of the steps (1 Kgs 10.18-20; 2 Chr 9.17-19). When administering justice, issuing royal orders, or granting an audience, the king occupied the throne (1 Kgs 2.19, 7.7, 10.18-20, 22.10). The throne of God is in heaven (Ps 11.4, 103.19; Isa 66.1; Mt 5.33-35) and he set up the throne of David (2 Sam 3.10) to be established forever (2 Sam 7.13; 1 Kgs 2.45; Ps 89.35-37). This prophecy (Isa 9.6,7; Jer 33.15-17) was fulfilled in Christ (Lk 1.31-33).

TIBERIAS. A city on the Sea of Galilee, built by Herod Antipas, and named after Tiberias who was then emperor. It was the capital of Galilee until the reign of Herod Agrippa II. The Sea of Galilee is also called the Sea of Tiberias (Jn 6.1, 21.1).

TIMOTHY. Paul's companion and assistant. A native of Lystra, Timothy was the child of a mixed marriage. His mother was Jewish, his father was Greek (Acts 16.1). He was given religious instruction at an early age by his mother, Eunice, and his grandmother, Lois (2 Tim 1.5, 3.15). To forestall criticism of Timothy on the part of the Jews, Paul caused him to be circumcised (Acts 16.3). He was the recipient of several of Paul's epistles.

TITHE. A tenth part of one's income. Abraham gave a tenth of the spoils of his victory to Melchizedek, the priest-king of Salem (Gen 14.20). Under the Mosiac law the Jews were required to give a tenth of the products of the soil and of cattle "to the Lord" (Lev 27.30,32). Of the cattle every tenth animal was set apart. The tithe was taken to the sanctuary where a portion was eaten by the giver and the Levites in a eucharistic feast and the balance went to the Levites. Every third year the tithe was stored in the town of the givers, and the widow, the stranger, the fatherless, and Levite could partake of it (Deut 14.28,29).

TITUS. A companion and fellow-laborer of Paul. A Christian convert of Greek parentage, he is first mentioned in the Bible when he accompanied Paul to Jerusalem where a church council considered the question of circumcision as it related to Gentile Christians. Titus was not required by the council to be circumcised (Gal 2.1-3). Paul's epistle to him was written to guide his activities in Crete (Titus 1.5-3.11).

TOMB. Caverns, both natural and artificial, were used by the Hebrews for the burial of their dead (Gen 23.9; Isa 22.16; Jn 11.38). To protect the tomb, a stone was placed against the entrance (Mt 27.60). Sepulchers were generally outside the city, and often on the face of a cliff some distance from the ground. It was often whitewashed so it could be clearly seen and not touched as contact with it would render one ceremonially unclean.

TONGUE. The organ of speech (Job 29.10; Ps 39.3, 71.24; Jas 3.6). It denotes the language or dialect of a people

(Esth 1.22; Dan 1.4; Acts 1.19, 2.4,8,11). In the story of the tower of Babel God purposely confuses the language of the people, causing the various peoples of the earth to understand only their own tongue, or language. This story explains the rise of all languages from a single origin (Gen 11.1-9). On the day of Pentecost, when the Holy Spirit descended, tongues of fire appeared and the Apostles began to speak as the spirit gave them utterance (Acts 2.1-21).

TRADITION. Precepts and rules, not in the written law but believed to have been given by God to Moses. Orally transmitted from generation to generation, they were to be obeyed with the same reverence as the law (Mt 15.2,3,6; Mk 7.3,5,9,13; Col 2.8).

TRANSFIGURATION. A moment in the life of Jesus in which, while on a high mountain with Peter, James, and John, he suddenly was visited by Moses and Elijah who spoke of his coming death (Lk 9.28-31). During this time his face shone brightly and his clothes appeared white as light (Mt 17.2). It was believed that the purpose of this visit was to prepare the disciples for the coming events which were to culminate in the crucifixion. The site of the transfiguration is thought to be Mount Hermon. After this event Jesus told the disciples to tell no one of the transfiguration until after the "Son of Man has been risen from the dead" (Mt. 17.9; Mk 9.9).

TYCHICUS. A fellow-laborer of the apostle Paul who went to Troas to await Paul's coming to that city at the close of the third journey (Acts 20.4). It was he who brought to the Ephesians and Colossians Paul's epistles (Eph 6.21; Col 4.7).

TYRE. A very ancient city of Phoenicia on a strongly protected island about half a mile from the shore. Its importance was frequently referred to by ancient writers (Ezek 26.1-27.32). In the time of David and Solomon very friendly relations existed. Hiram, king of Tyre, furnished David with materials and craftsmen for his palace (2 Sam

5.11). He also provided materials for Solomon's Temple and other building enterprises (1 Kgs 5.1; 9.10-14; 2 Chr 2.3,11). Jesus once came to the coasts of Tyre and Sidon (Mt 15.21-31; Mk 7.24-31). A Christian Church was founded at Tyre and here Paul spent some time (Acts 21.3,4).

U

UNCLEAN ANIMALS. According to Mosaic law unclean animals—those unfit for food—included: 1. Those who do not have cloven hooves and do not chew the cud (Lev 11.3-8); hence all carnivorous and most other animals except oxen, sheep, goats, and certain deer and gazelles (Deut 14.4-8). 2. Carnivorous birds (Lev 11.13-19; Deut 14.12-18). 3. Water animals which lack either fins or scales, notably eels (Lev 11.9-12). 4. Insects not provided with leaping legs similar to those of a locust (Lev 11.20-23). 5. All creeping things, including certain small quadrupeds (Lev 11.29-31,41-43).

URIAH. One of David's warriors, a Hittite (2 Sam 23.39; 1 Chr 11.41). He was the husband of Bathsheba, with whom David committed adultery. As a result David had Uriah placed in a dangerous position in the line of battle and Uriah was killed. David then married Bathsheba (2 Sam 1.1-27; Mt 1.6).

UZZAH. When the ark was on its way to Jerusalem in the reign of David, it was jolted by the stumbling of the oxen. Uzzah put forth his hand to steady it and was struck dead. The place was called Perez-uzzah, meaning the breaking out against Uzzah (2 Sam 6.3-8; 1 Chr 13.7-14).

V

VERSIONS. Translations of the whole or parts of the Bible into languages other than the original.

VINE. By this word is usually denoted the grape vine (Gen

40.9-11; Ps 78.47). Palestine was very favorable to the growth of the vine, especially in the hill country (Num 13.23; Judg 9.27, 21.20; Jer 31.5). The vintage was a festive season and was attended with singing and shouting as the grapes were trodden in the press (Isa 16.10; Jer 25.30, 48.33). Jesus compared himself to the vine and his disciples to the branches (Jn 15.1-8).

VISIONS. An order of mental phenomena in which God communicated to the mind in accordance with the mind's constitution. The genuineness of visions containing predictions was established by the fulfillment of the predictions. Those who falsely declared they had received visions were denounced (Jer 14.14, 23.16; Ezek 13.7). Dreams should be distinguished from visions.

VOW. A promise to God to perform some service for him on condition that he, in return grant a specific favor, such as a safe journey (Gen 28.20-22), victory (Judg 11.30,31), or offspring (1 Sam 1.11). A more disinterested vow was made by the Nazarite who sought God's good will, in return for which he promised to give up strong drink, cutting his hair, and to dedicate himself wholly to the Lord (Num 6.1-21).

W

WAVE OFFERING. A portion of the peace offering dedicated to the priest. During the wave offering the breast of the sacrificed animal was waved to and fro as it was carried toward the altar by the priest. This symbolized its presentation to the Lord and the Lord's return of it to the priests (Ex 29.19-28; Lev 7.28-36, 10.12,15). At harvest time a sheaf of firstfruits was waved on the second day of the passover, thereby dedicating the harvest to the Lord (Lev 23.10,11).

WEEKS, FEAST OF. One of the three annual feasts at which time all the men of Israel were required to present themselves at the sanctuary (Ex 34.22,23). It fell seven weeks after the waving of the sheaf and is also called Pentecost (Acts 2.1) or the feast of harvest because the first fruits of the wheat harvest were presented (Ex 23.16, 34.22; Num 28.26).

WIDOW. Because of the helpless position of widows, the Mosiac law required that they be kindly treated. Those who disregarded this law were to be punished (Deut 10.18, 24.17, 19, 27.19; Zech 7.10-12; Mal 3.5; Mk 12.40). Some Hebrew widows were cared for by their children or their relatives (Gen 38.11) or had the means to support themselves (Judg 17.1-6). In addition, a brother-in-law or close relative could be required to marry a young and childless widow (Deut 25.5-10; Ruth 4.1-13). However, those widows who had no family, or whose relatives were poor, were in a very difficult position. Ruth, for example, gleaned the field after the reapers to support herself and Naomi (Ruth 2.2,17,18). In the early church care for the widows was a duty of the congregation and provisions were made to cover their needs (Acts 6.1; 1 Tim 5.3-16; Jas 1.27).

WINE. The Hebrew word *Yayim* is used to denote wine or fermented grape juice and its intoxicating character is obvious from the Scriptural use of the word. Palestine was a wine-producing country, and wine was commonly used. Lot drank wine and became intoxicated (Gen 19.32). The priests were forbidden to use wine during their sacred ministrations (Lev 10.9) and the Nazarite, during the period of his vow, had to abstain from wine as well as from eating of grapes (Num 6.3,4). The Scriptures set forth in striking forms the effects of the intemperate use of wine. Some of these effects are the enslavement of the drinker to wine (Hos 4.11), the redness of the eye (Gen 49.12), improper speech (Prov 20.1, 23.29-32; (Isa 28.7), distorted judgment (Prov 31.5). What was used by Jesus in the institution of the Lord's Supper is called the "fruit of the vine" (Mt 26.29). Paul told Timothy to take a little wine for the sake of his stomach (1 Tim 5.23).

WISDOM. The ability to judge fairly and to understand and make wise use of facts. The Hebrew conception was that wisdom is an attribute of God (Job 28; Isa 40.12-14; Rom 11.33-35) and that he shared it with certain men (Prov 2.1-22; Eccl 2.26; 1 Cor 2.4-12, 12.7,8; Eph 1.17; Col 1.9). The portion of the Bible, known as wisdom literature, consists of Job, Proverbs, Ecclesiastes, Song of Solomon. Paul condemned worldly wisdom (1 Cor 1.19-31; Col 2.8; 1 Tim 6.20).

WITNESS. 1. A memorial to an event. One such witness was the heap of stones set up by Jacob and Laban in witness of their covenant (Gen 31.46-52). Joshua set up a stone in witness of his covenant with the people of Israel (Josh 24.27). 2. A person who gave testimony, especially in legal matters. Witnesses were needed to attest a property transaction or a betrothal (Ruth 4.9; Jer 32.10). Under Mosaic law, in criminal cases, it was necessary to have two witnesses (Deut 17.6; Mt 18.16). If it were discovered that a witness had given false testimony, then he was punished with the same penalty the accused would have drawn (Deut 19.16-19). In carrying out a death sentence the witnesses were the first to cast the stones (Deut 17.6,7; 1 Kgs 21.10). 3. One who testifies to his faith in Christ (Lk 24.48; Heb 12.1). The Greek word for witness is martyr, a word that came to denote one who had suffered death rather than abandon his faith (Acts 22.20; Rev 2.13).

WOMAN. In her creation she was the helpmeet and equal of man (Gen 2.21-24). In early times women labored in the fields and took care of sheep (Gen 29.6, Ex 2.16; Ruth 2.3,8) but their main duties were of a household nature such as grinding grain (Mt 24.41), caring for the physical needs of the family (1 Sam 2.19; 2 Sam 13.8; Prov 31.13,19; Acts 9.36-39), supervising the home (1 Tim 5.14), and instructing the children (Prov 1.8, 31.1; 2 Tim 3.15). Under the Mosaic law the wife and mother was respected and honored (Ex 20.12, Prov 1.8; 18.22; Eccl 9.9). In the New Testament she was further ennobled by Jesus through his teachings on adultery, marriage, and divorce (Mt 5.27-32) and through his attitude toward his mother, the sisters at Bethany, and the woman at the well (Lk 10.38-42; Jn 4.7-30, 19.25-27).

WORSHIP. Religious reverence and homage, especially the act of paying divine honor to God (Ex 34:14, Mt 4.10). Temple worship, besides featuring sacrifice, was highly ritualistic as evidenced by its use of the Psalms. Synagoge worship after the Exile and through New Testament times made of prime importance the reading of the law and the prophets (Lk 4.14-21). Early Christian worship included preaching, prayer, reading of scripture, singing, administration of the Lord's Supper, and almsgiving (Acts 12.5, 20.7; 1 Cor 11.18-29, 16.1,2; Col 3.16; 1 Thess 5.27).

Y

YOKE. A transverse wooden bar fashioned to fit the necks of two draft animals, usually oxen. Attached to it is the pole of the plow or vehicle to be drawn (Num 19.2; 1 Kgs 19.19). The word is used figuratively of bondage and servitude (Deut 28.48; Mt 11.28-30; Acts 15.10; Gal 5.1; 1 Tim 6.1).

Z

ZACCHAEUS A chief publican who had charge of the revenues of the distrtict of Jericho (Lk 19.1-10).

ZACHARIAH. Father of John the Baptist. He was a priest of the course of Abia (Lk 1.5). His wife, Elizabeth, was related to the mother of Jesus. While he was engaged in burning incense at the hour of prayer, an angel assured him that his prayer for a son was answered. On account of the age of Elizabeth he was doubtful and asked for a sign. As a result he became dumb until John was born. When he spoke, he praised God (Lk 1.18-22,62-64).

ZEBULUN. 1. The youngest of the sons of Jacob by Leah

(Gen 30.19,20). 2. Tribe of Zebulun. Its territory was in the northern section between the Mediterranean and the Sea of Galilee. Within its bounds were Nazareth and Cana.

ZION. One of the hills of Jerusalem. It was west of Kidron Valley and south of the Temple area. Upon it was the ancient stronghold of the Jebusites, renamed the city of David (2 Sam 5.7, 1 Chr 11.5). The name Zion was extended to include the Temple area and sometimes the whole of Jerusalem (Ps 48, 65.1, 102.21; Isa 2.3, 8.18). Heaven is called Zion (Heb 12.22; Rev 14.1), symbol of the spiritual Zion, the city of God.